Growing
Wild

Growing Wild

K.P. RENNIE

ISBN: 978-1-6581-1334-2

DISCLAIMER

This is a work of nonfiction. The events are portrayed to the best of my ability. Many of these words came from journals I kept when I was 14, some of the names and identifying details have been changed to protect the privacy of others.

We all did the best we could at the time.

I'm going to live in Heaven with Jesus if everybody be's mean at me. Every time people are mean at me I'm going to live someplace else. Tomorrow after dinner I'm going and I'll take all my things with me.

Karen- age 3 ½

CONTENTS

1 • THE FIVE HEADED MONSTER OF EXCELSIOR

MAY 15 1982 ▪**Fifteen years old**

Three minutes ago, I was in the living room snuggled under a blanket with Sherman, my stuffed elephant.

The house is quiet, and feels unusually cold. There is a note on the table to my brother: *"We'll be back in a few days. Here is money for pizza."*

Grabbing my pad of paper and pen I write, *"Mom, where you going?"* and walk outside. My parents stop me at the front steps, cornering me in the entryway. I show Mom the pad.

"Not me," she says. "We."

Flipping to the next page of the notebook, I cover it with a giant question mark.

"We are all going." Her voice is cold, factual, devoid of emotion.

I hold out the notebook and tap on the question mark.

"We are all going to check out that school in Colorado."

"No!" I try to scream, but laryngitis prevents my fury from being audible. As I write the question, "Why?" on my pad, my dad grabs my arm and says,

"Karen, get in the van."

Shaking my head no, I turn to run back into the house. They grab me, one on each side, and start pulling me towards the van. I scream but little sound comes out. The van door opens and my mom's friend, Diana, is sitting in the back of the van. Despite my best fight, they win. I'm trapped in the van and as we back out of the driveway I yell at Diana "Fuck you, bitch!" My voice is barely a whisper. She hears me.

Crawling under the pile of blankets and pillows on the floor of the van, I try to escape the cold and them. We are all happy to pretend I am invisible under the blanket; I curl up in a ball and wish they would never find me. I take out an earring and prick away at the skin on my wrist.

1

Kids in school sometimes do the "eraser dare"—rubbing an eraser back and forth across their skin to see who stops first. Eventually the skin rips open and I heard people have bled out because the skin has been rubbed too thin to stitch. I pray it's true, it's all I've got. My parents will think I've gone back to sleep. I will be dead before the blood seeps out from under the blanket.

My wrist burns. It's raw but it doesn't look anywhere near ready to open up and bleed out. I try to stab the vein with the earring, puncture it a few times. Nothing works. If I had a razor blade, two quick slices and this could all be over. The van's tires continue rolling, creating distance between me and everything familiar.

I peer out from under the blankets. My dad has joined my mom in the front seat. Diana is still sitting in back with me. I could get up and launch myself out the back door before anyone had a chance to stop me. But what if I didn't die? What if I only broke a few bones? That wouldn't stop them from taking me to this boarding school. And what if I did permanent damage, left incapacitated and dependent on them forever? What if I am left without even having the option of suicide? My mom always says, "Suicide is never an option," but I think about it all the time. I had a thousand miles to think of nothing but suicide, or escape.

We travel two days for my parents to leave me somewhere none of us have ever seen.

Our destination is a big, red brick building, the word "Excelsior!" written in bold, black letters down one of the glass entry doors. Inside, a teenager is at the front desk, but before we make it to her post we are intercepted by a beefy woman wearing men's blue Dickies work pants. She looks like the female version of our neighbor who works for the probation department. Ms. Dickies leads us to a huge, proper conference room where several other adults are waiting. The brawny woman sits on the edge of her seat; I'm not sure if she is uncertain she will fit between the arms of the chair, or if she is naturally on edge. There are ashtrays on the table. I grab one of my dad's Marlboros and his lighter as we sit. The adults begin to talk, intentionally leaving me out of the conversation, like I'm a little girl;- they don't want me to understand what they are saying, but know they can't spell out the undesirable or complicated words in front of me. I want to look at the pamphlets my parents are flipping through, but they don't pass them over to me. Doesn't this involve me? What's with the secrecy? I decide to force my way into the conversation.

"My best friend attends boarding school in Ojai Valley; it seemed like a pretty cool place when I went to her graduation."

The adults look at me funny—like I'm missing something. My

parents stand when they are invited to take a tour. I'm told to wait where I am with Ms. Dickies, my unofficial babysitter.

This woman in man's clothing isn't making a big effort to talk with me. We sit for a few minutes before I realize my dad's taken his cigarettes. As I get up and head to the van, the big babysitter asks "What do you think you're doing?"

"I'm going to the van to get my smokes. My dad took his."

"No, you aren't," she barks.

"The van is right outside, be right back." I step out of the conference room and the door closes behind me.

Alarms scream from speakers in the ceiling, people are running, there is commotion all around me. I never make it back to the door that reads "Excelsior!"

I'm surrounded by people I don't recognize- none of these faces were in the conference room, except the Dickies lady who isn't visible, but I can hear her massive voice barking orders. My parents aren't anywhere around; they don't come when I scream for their help. I am taken down, one person at each limb and another at my head. None of the people restraining me have uniforms or badges- how do they have any authority or reason to do this? As they drag me down a hallway, I writhe and scream for help and bite at hands that grip tightly at my wrists.

"Stop Biting!" they say, "Calm down!"

"Let me go!" I reply. "Who the hell are you?"

Voices yell for me to be quiet. My vision fills with bright lights and unfamiliar faces, I randomly notice panels missing from the dirty drop ceiling. Bodies block my periphery; I can only see upwards, like I'm falling into a well- or hell.

"Where are my parents?" Nobody answers; they are like a five-headed monster working in unison to drag me down. It's as if they planned this all along and have done it a hundred times before.

They toss me onto a mattress and the last limb of the five-headed monster locks the door behind them. Typically such a soft, innocent sound, but this time the lock is keeping me prisoner, rather than protecting me from the monsters outside. That click was the sound of my freedom stolen. The room immediately shrinks.

The door that locked between the monster and me has a rectangular window about the size of a shoebox. I hit it hard and it doesn't budge. I'm trapped. I can't believe my eyes because my mind is confused. Looking but never seeing, I can't grasp this reality.

All the walls are white, not padded with soft squishy quilt stuff like you see in movies or read about, instead lined in ugly Formica so if you ram your head into the walls they give way just enough to not cause any "real" damage. The plastic is white with flecks of gray and gold. A design left over from the 1960's- too ugly to be cool or vintage- it looks cheap and dirty. This Formica wainscoting runs the perimeter of the room and is a little taller than me; a five foot 14 year old. Assuming most of the prisoners kept in this room are about my size only makes this place more horrific to think about.

Hard plastic caps the top of the Formica. No matter how hard I try, running my finger over the length of it, walking in circles around the room again and again, there is no way to dislodge a piece of the endless plastic with no beginning. Eventually I give up on my idea to somehow break a piece off to hurt someone, or better, myself.

The mattress on the floor is naked in the barren room like a sacrificial altar; no pillow, sheets, box spring or frame. I lie down and cry into it. I beat the shit out of it. I yell and curse at the world from that stained, lumpy mattress- but hours later, no one comes.

In the movies, when people are trapped in jail, there are always bars on the window. As a viewer you have plenty of time to fabricate elaborate plans on how you could defeat those bars; they are always wide apart, fragile, accessible to your allies in the outside world. The window in this room doesn't have bars, but wire mesh, thick as a #2 pencil. The screening has spaces open no wider than ¾ inch square. The most you can push through that cold metal lattice would be a Starburst candy and you'd have to take the wrapper off and utilize its pliability. If I did manage to squeeze the candy through, it would fall two stories to its death.

Looking out the window to the weird industrial area below, I see a few girls around my age, get into a van with an adult and drive away. I hope they are escaping but they don't look to be in a hurry. Electric shock à la "One Flew Over the Cuckoo's Nest" comes to mind. Are these kids now like zombies, shadows of what they once were? If this is a boarding school, like my parents said, where are the horses, the ceramics classes, the other kids? There are no sounds of happy school children frolicking in the distance. I watch out the window and listen carefully and never see the girls return in the van.

Every hour or so, someone looks in through the mesh enforced window in the door.

I yell "Where are my parents?"

They ask "Do you need to use the restroom?"

If I say yes, 3 people are on guard to escort me across the hall and lock me in the bathroom. There's nothing in the bathroom to devise a spectacular James Bond/MacGyver escape. No windows or mirror, only a sink and a toilet. I unroll long strips of toilet paper and twist them together, wondering how many layers it would take to make a rope strong enough to hang myself. Only moments later they are knocking on the door telling me to hurry up or they are coming in. I am escorted the few steps back to the room and the door is locked behind me again. After a few trips to the bathroom, my entourage is reduced to one escort. They know I can't escape and they can see that I am starting to know that too. It reminds me of that term I've never liked — "breaking a horse".

Eventually someone brings food in on a beige partitioned cafeteria tray. I can't imagine ever enjoying food or even eating again. At the end of the day another meal is delivered. When that tray, still full, is removed, I am given a blanket and pillow. My parents haven't come to say goodbye or explain themselves. As the evening starts to suck the sunlight from the room I have to consider the idea that my parents aren't faking; they won't be coming back to get me. Why hasn't anyone come to explain my fate? No pamphlets with guidelines, no campus tour, no crudely made orientation film. I am blind and unknowing.

I am a fucking victim. When Jack kicked me and cracked my ribs I was able to make sense of it. He had a reason. I could fight back. It was one against one. No one is hugging me now and saying they are sorry. I want comfort from my parents; I want a promise that things will be better.

My mom and dad obviously don't love me- they discarded me here with the monster and might be halfway home already. I think of Jack and how much he loves me; how he never demands anything of me. I could do or be whoever I want; his love for me is unconditional. He loves me no matter who I sleep with. My parents couldn't love me because I slept with him. Jack is probably thinking of me right now, looking at my initials tattooed on his arm, I fall asleep certain of his love for me.

My nightmare is I am kidnapped and locked away. I wake to the horror that this is my reality. I swear tears are coming before I am fully awake. My face is wet, did my crying wake me up? Sweat covers me and I'm chilled to the bone. On a mattress, flat on the floor, I may as well be on a raft in the middle of the ocean. A loud scream rips from my throat, so much bigger than I expected because I feel so small. I scream again and it makes me feel stronger. I revel in my voice and feel like I have launched some small attack on my captors. An adult I've never seen before comes in and stands over me. My verbal attack has ended. She doesn't have to explain, she wins the moment she used a key to get in.

"You've just earned a zero for your behavior," she announces.

"What the fuck are you talking about?" I ask kindly.

"And another one for language." She adds to my punishment, and confusion.

"What are you keeping score for?" I truly don't know. "Zero plus zero is still zero"

"And another one for attitude".

She is creative and attentive, I'll give her that. Sometimes I know when to shut up and I've decided now would be a good time. This old chubby face that hasn't worn a smile in a decade, would happily pull the pin out of another zero grenade. She seems genuinely disappointed that she can't bomb me again as she backs out of the room and locks the door.

I cry. I cry through all the clichés: I cry a river, an ocean, til there are no more tears, til I can't cry anymore. I cry until my face hurts, my head hurts, my heart hurts. It's possible if I stop crying I will completely turn to stone and become rotten and evil like the monsters that have me caged. My tears are the only thing they don't have control of.

(In my mind Johnny Thunders commiserates with me. I can hear him singing)

♫ It doesn't pay to try,
All the smart boys know why,
It doesn't mean I didn't try,
I just never know why.
Feels so cold and all alone,
'Cause baby, you're not at home.
And when I'm home
Big deal, I'm still alone.
You can't put your arms around a memory
So don't try. ♫

Anonymous adult, number who-knows, arrives with a saccharine smile and another tray of beige.

"You may as well take that with you. I don't want it."

"If you don't eat some of your meal, you will get a zero," she says, still smiling.

"Fuck you! What are you going to do then? Lock me up or take away my food?"

It feels good to yell some more; I've decided anger is more comfortable than sadness. At least anger gives me energy; sadness sucks the life from me. I stare at the tray of food on the floor and listen to the door lock behind me, the Clash song "Clampdown" playing in the background of my mind.

♫ Let fury have the hour,
Anger can be power,

Did you know that you can use it?
The voices in your head are calling,
Stop wasting your time, there's nothing coming,
Only a fool would think someone could save you. ♫

The passing of time is marked by the sound of school bells in the distance, and the rotating trays of beige in my cage. I try to communicate telepathically with Jack to tell him I love him. I try to send messages through the bond I am supposed to have with my mom to come and get me out. I don't know if anyone is listening. No paper to write or draw and clear my head, no music to soothe my soul. The sun rises and falls, while strangers look in and check in and lock me in. Food is delivered and removed. Blankets and pillows arrive and depart like soft friends, I wish they could stay and visit longer. Sometimes I can hear the sound of the T.V. from another room, but not enough to decipher any words. I can make out the sound of other girls' voices but I don't know how many. Occasionally I catch a glimpse of a girl my age looking through the little window in the door, but they walk away the second I look up. The only thing worse than trying to fall asleep after being in a room all day by yourself is waking up to another day in that same room. My life is on a tape loop.

Random adult, number whatever, comes in with breakfast. This time she leaves the door open behind her. She knows my spirit has been broken and I'm not going to try to escape anymore.

"You have been in T.L.C. for three days. Don't you want to come out of this room?"

"I don't even know what T.L.C. is, and how can I come out of this room when you people keep locking me in?"

"T.L.C. stands for The Learning Center and you are here with other high risk girls. If you behave yourself, you can come join the group today, maybe even go to the cafeteria by the end of the week."

"At risk for what?"

"For running, for destructive behavior and for negatively influencing others". She has an explanation for everything, none of which make sense to me.

"How do you know all this when you don't even know me? I've been locked in this room for days." I don't know why I attempt to explain myself to them. As if convincing them they made a mistake will result in being sent home.

"It took five staff members to bring you in here, so you are obviously a flight risk."

"I was only going to get my cigarettes!"

"You aren't allowed to smoke in T.L.C." She delivers a sinister

Cheshire smile, knowing she isn't making any sense. She doesn't have to.

"I wasn't in T.L.C. I thought I was in a conference room at a boarding school. I am two days drive away from home. I don't have any idea where I am. Where would I run to?" It would be great if her answer included a bus schedule and fare.

"When you are prepared to behave, you can come out of the room and take a shower, and meet the other girls in the unit."

It hasn't been explained what "behaving" means, other than to quit hitting the walls and cussing out the people in charge.

Down a narrow hall is a bathroom with one shower stall in it, folded clothes and a clean towel are stacked on a stool. The woman who escorted me says "I'll wait right here" stands in the doorway and turns her back to me. I undress quickly and get in the shower, It feels good to stand under the warm water; I haven't had a shower since my parents threw me in the van over six days ago. For a moment, with my eyes closed and the water running down my neck, the situation feels almost normal.

After the shower, I'm escorted past the room that has held me in isolation, and into the dark, sad, gloom of the T.L.C. common room.

There is one double locked door on the opposite wall, and no windows. No means of escape as far as I can figure at first glance. Three girls momentarily assess me and then go back to staring at the T.V. tucked into the left corner of the room. I do my best to avoid eye contact with them, and survey the room instead. There is a faded orange and brown chair upholstered with something the texture of burlap, left over from the early 1970's. Along the entirety of the wall an ugly black vinyl couch sits arm-to-arm with a chair. There's barely enough room to walk between the couch and a low coffee table. Beyond the coffee table is a bookshelf cluttered with books and board games. Judging from the condition of the boxes, it's unlikely the board games have all their pieces or that game night is a common occurrence. On the right side of the hall doorway a big desk clearly defines the space as their turf; none of the kids are allowed on that side. One staff member has 40% of the room. The four of us girls in T.L.C. have the other 60%.

I sit in the only open space available next to a Mexican girl maybe two years older than me. She's only a little bigger than I am; with long thick brown hair down the middle of her flannel clad back. She has a baby face with jet black eyes: cold and lifeless like a doll. There is no delineation between the pupil and iris.

"I'm Jeanette. Probation violation."

"K.P." I say, unsure of what other clarifiers I should provide. Below one of her black armor eyes is a tattoo of a tiny number 13.

"I like that tattoo." I can't imagine ever tattooing my face, but it seems to suit her, the tattoo looks like a beauty mark.

"Third gen. East thirteen"

"I have no clue what that means. I'm not from Colorado."

She just laughs and shakes her head. I notice that she has three dots tattooed on the space between her thumb and pointer finger.

"What's that?" I ask, pointing to her hand.

"Mi Vida Loca."

"What does that mean?"

"My crazy life. My mom is in lock-up for parole violation, we should get out at the same time."

I can't tell if Jeanette is happy or sad about this. No matter what her face, body or words say, her eyes hide all emotion. That is her superpower; she will always keep people guessing. Those eyes make me afraid and in awe. She is only 16 years old, but I would guess the staff is a little afraid of her. Yes; "My crazy life".

"Why is your hair so short and yellow?" Jeanette asks.

"I'm a punk."

Our conversation is interrupted by the adult du jour who tells me one of the ways for me to "behave" is to not identify myself as "Punk Rock".

"But she asked me about my hair."

"You will need to find another way to answer."

How can Jeanette sit here and talk about her crimes, her tattoos, her gang affiliation, her probation, her mother's criminal activity — and the only control over our conversation comes when I mention punk rock? How can music, an art form, be so much more offensive?

How can I be worse than her?

"I heard it took five staff to drag you in here."

"How did you get put in here?" I asked.

"I got bussed here after court."

After we talk I'm aware of the most important difference between Jeanette and me: her family would have her back if they could.

When the girls leave T.L.C. to go to the cafeteria and then to school, I'm left with a yearning for company that may never be satisfied after so many days in solitude. It's like someone pulled the scab right off of the wound. The adult left behind to guard me talks about what's on the other side of the door: Several dorms called cottages that house other girls. Eventually when I "earn the privilege" to leave T.L.C. they will "place" me in the appropriate cottage.

"What do I have to do to move to a cottage?" I want answers.

"We have to see a change in you."

"Like what? What kind of change? What can I do?"

"It's nothing specific. There is no formula, it's a process." They don't have the answer, they don't know what they want, it's all bullshit.

I'm given a notebook and a weird little felt tip pen, slightly longer than my index finger.

"You can go back to your room now and start writing."

"Start writing what?"

"For the remainder of your stay here, you will write in a journal for 30 minutes a day. In addition, you will complete an autobiography as soon as possible, so we can get to know you better."

2 • AUTOBIOGRAPHY

You lock me in a room and demand I write a story about my life so *you* can know *me* better. Who are you? I don't know anything about you people. Fuck you for locking me up taking me away from the only person who ever loved me and the only group where I ever belonged.

Did you consider maybe I ran away from home to save myself? I needed to get away before they make <u>me</u> crazy? My parents are not going to be okay until they hear me say that it's my fault that their home life sucks. But everything is not my fault.

You don't even know who I am. You can't see me. How can I write a fucking autobiography locked in a room? You have made the story of my life come to a complete stop!—I am not "living my life" I am barely allowed to exist in it.

Things keep going around in circles–I'm not to be trusted because I run away or if I can't get away I cut myself. So my parents put me on restriction, on probation, locked in my room, but then I'm sad, depressed, angry, so I cut myself because I can't get away—and the cycle starts again.

Now you say I have to change on the inside or I will continue to be locked up – but no one will tell me how! I want to be left alone. I want to be loved and accepted and the only person who has done that has been Jack. Why is it so hard for my parents to let me go if they don't like me anyway? My autobiography—what a joke. Fuck you all.

—Karen, that language will not be tolerated here. Every girl here writes an autobiography and you will too. Start with a story that has affected you profoundly. We would like to know more about your relationship with your parents and boyfriend, as well as your first experiences with cigarettes, alcohol, drugs and sex. Your compliance with this task is one of the ways that you can show you are trying to cooperate and change. —Staff

3 • FIRST KISS

1972 ▪Four years old

My first kiss was with Vincent Vasquez. We hid behind the shed that held the sandbox supplies. I was excited to tell my parents when I got home, thinking they would want to know everything about him, about the moment. I'm more excited to tell my parents at dinner than I was to kiss him in the morning, but I learned. I learned not to tell my parents anything, or they get angry.

–Karen, This assignment is not for you to accuse and blame your parents.–Staff

1975 ▪Eight years old

My next first kiss was with Andy when I was eight. He was an out of town house guest and I had a crush. Alone at my dad's construction site, he tried to teach me how to French kiss. I found it disgusting, but figured he knew much more than I did, after all, he was eighteen. I never told my parents, wanting to avoid their anger.

Karen– You seem to be making light of these experiences and this writing assignment. We want to know about major events in your life, you will continue writing until we do. –Staff

Because I never discussed this with my parents, it was never a major event. It was nothing. It was what my dad would call a "non-issue".

13

4 ● FIRST CIGARETTE

1978 ▪Eleven years old

Audrey and I make the one and a half mile walk from Seaside Elementary to our suburban block. She is my only friend since we moved into our incomplete construction site house three months ago. Her brother, Curtis, is the same age as me, and Audrey is two years younger, which makes her eight.

Hanging out at Audrey's house is great but I have to lie about it. My mom's rule is that I'm not allowed in anyone's house unless an adult is home. Audrey's dad, Terry, is never home and she only sees her mom on the weekends. We hang out on Audrey's front yard but often sneak inside. My dad is always working on our house while I am down the street. My mom works late every night trying to pay for the construction.

Walking home, Audrey's house comes into view at the crest of the first hill on our street. Her dad looks lost even though he's sitting right there on the steps of his own front door. He grabs a Ritz cracker out of the box and smears cream cheese on it, stuffing the whole thing in his mouth at once. There is a shiny new black Porsche on his bumpy, broken asphalt driveway. Audrey starts running towards the driver—her mom who is wearing a tube top, Dolphin shorts, visor and big sunglasses—she looks like one of Charlie's Angels. Audrey gives her mom a big long hug. Audrey never talks to me about why her parents got divorced, but it seems hard on her not having both her parents around.

I can't remember the last time I saw my parents in the same room together, or when I last ran up and hugged my mom. Lately I have been wishing my parents would get divorced. They really don't seem to like each other. Having divorced parents seems like less of a hassle, fewer people watching over you, fewer people to answer to, but I guess that's not reality because Audrey is holding onto her mom tightly. Curtis has an angry look on his face and will only look at his mom from the wrong side of his bedroom window.

"Maybe it's time you end this surprise visit and head back to Newport Beach" Terry tells his ex-wife. "I've got a softball game to get to."

"Maybe you can get our son to come out and give me a kiss goodbye?" she retorts, kissing her daughter and promising to pick her up on the weekend.

"I'm sure if he wanted to kiss you, he would."

She drives off in her tiny car, her leather Gucci bag and tennis racket riding shotgun.

"Time to go check in with my dad," I tell them.

"Isn't it cold in that big house with all those holes in the walls?" Terry teases me.

"We don't use any of those rooms yet. We all sleep in the only room that's done. My dad is working on the kitchen now so we don't have to eat pizza all the time."

"I'm only kidding you, that house looks like it's going to be huge if it ever gets done." Terry hands me a Ritz cracker with cream cheese.

"It's not that big—it only has three bedrooms—but it has two living rooms."

"What do you need two living rooms for?" It's not the first time I've heard that question.

"So the grownups can get away from the kids." I repeat my parent's answer.

Walking up to the top of the second hill and into our construction zone home, I know my mom will be mad when I see my dad hasn't worked on the kitchen at all. He tells me he is about to drywall the downstairs hallway and bathroom.

"There will be some sanding work for you to do in a few days. You can stay out and play today."

On my way out of the house I glance at my piano—it looks misplaced against the skeleton of raw 2x4's that will someday be walls. Pulling off the tarp and sitting at it, I begin to play Beethoven's Moonlight Sonata. I love how it sounds in the giant empty construction site of our future living and dining rooms. The sound echoes in the hollow room—no carpet or drywall to absorb the sound. I imagine playing at a hall on a grand piano. I haven't finished playing the piece when my dad interrupts mid-song.

"Cover up the piano up before drywall dust gets in between the keys."

Why couldn't he let me finish? It's one of the few songs I can play perfectly still, after not taking lessons for years. Whatever—I'm happy to leave and walk back down to Audrey's house. "Checking in" with dad is a complete waste of time.

Terry is wearing his softball uniform, making hamburger mixed with boxed macaroni and cheese for dinner. Curtis and his friend Lee wait for dinner. Lee is cool, he has long, black feathered hair and puka shells. He reminds me of the bad kid with the motorcycle in the movie "The Bad News Bears".

"You kids get in the house before its dark, I'll be calling you from the pizza parlor after the game." He kisses both of his kids on their foreheads. He kind of rumples my hair as he walks past me. It makes me feel like I belong.

When Terry leaves, Audrey and I put on the Fleetwood Mac *Rumors* album and practice our dance routine. We want to perform on the Gong Show to win prize money. Audrey will probably become famous and loved by the world. I want the prize money to buy a pet monkey so I can love it. We rehearse over and over to the song "Never Going Back Again." I think we're ready to perform, but I still can't get my parents' permission to go on the show.

After a while we make the living room dark. The shades are drawn and the lights are out. Even though it's late afternoon it feels like nighttime and we are pretending we're in a nightclub. Audrey's short red nails lay the needle down onto the *Saturday Night Fever* album. The Bee Gees start singing and Audrey starts dancing. Her hips trace infinity as her hands lift her hair up off her neck and then she lets it fall down again. Even though she's only eight years old she dances real sexy and moves around like a gypsy belly dancer. I like to watch her move—she is graceful and already like a teenager. Most of the time it seems like Audrey is older than me even though she's two years younger. My mom says she's "streetwise". Maybe it's because she is always on her own, or because her mom is so into dating and makeup. Lee comes in from the bedroom and starts dancing with Audrey. He's 14 years old, it's kind of weird with her being six years younger but there's only two girls and two boys in here and Audrey sure isn't gonna dance like that with her brother.

I don't mind Curtis, but I'm not in love with him. He wants to make out on the couch, so I sit and let him press his lips against mine. I want to pretend we are grown-ups at a disco, like playing house. Instead we have our eyes closed and he's making moaning sounds, so I make moaning sounds. He starts to move his head back and forth a little, so I move mine from side to side, our lips are smashed together—humming.

I don't see what the big deal is, all this kissing. Curtis' mood is changing and it's bugging me, frustrating me, because I'm not keeping up. I'm not feeling the same way he is from this kissing. His hands are everywhere— up and down my arms, my sides, up and down my legs. He should rub my back or my knees, rub the places where there is pain to make me feel better, not the places he wants to rub to make *him* feel better. He tries to touch my boobs but I push his hands away, embarrassed. I don't feel the way he does; I'm not sure he feels the way he is acting, I think he's faking the whole thing.

Opening my eyes to watch Audrey and Lee dance, they look like they're not faking anything. Audrey is writhing against him the same way I move when I'm alone squeezing my pillow between my legs. When she kisses Lee her lips aren't closed, they part open slightly and their mouths are wet. Maybe if I was kissing Lee; maybe if he was kissing me in that way I would feel different? Maybe if I was kissing Audrey I would feel different?

"Do you guys want to do the hustle?" I ask, wanting to get Curtis to stop grabbing at me, wishing for someone's attention besides his. Lee looks at Curtis and laughs. Curtis looks at me: mad. Curtis pushes away from me, gets up and comes back with some of his dad's pot.

"Come on Lee, let's go get stoned."

Lee kisses Audrey again and then walks out to the backyard with Curtis.

"Want to put on makeup?" Audrey asks me.

She switches gears so quickly I have to think she was faking the whole thing too. I would be mad if Lee left my side so quickly to go smoke pot with Curtis instead.

Audrey and I go in her room and plug in the curling iron to feather our hair and do our makeup. We are pretending to be grown-ups in our own apartment getting ready for a date.

Her door crashes open and Lee and Curtis barge into the room— they are mad for no reason. I guess that's what pot does to you. We're telling them to leave and yelling at them and screaming but they don't listen. They want to make out some more. Audrey starts screaming "No! Get out NOW! God DAMMIT!" Audrey is even better at swearing than I am. We sort of push them out of the room and then we push the bed up against the door so they can't come back in.

When I see them coming in through the window from the backyard, I feel like I'm in a movie; I'm caught up in the drama of it. We've trapped ourselves in by pushing the bed up against her door, they are standing at the window. They seem so much bigger now. "Knock it off!" I yell. I don't want to pretend with them. I don't wanna play along.

They are on a rampage of swearing and thrashing stuff in the room. Audrey and I grab the bed frame and pull— trying to get out of the room. We get pushed onto the bed and up against the door. We are cornered.

Audrey is hurt. Her head banged against the wall and she's crying real tears. This isn't a game. We aren't acting out a part we've seen in so many grown-up movies on T.V. My friend is hurt and I want this to stop now so I'm flying towards Lee in a rage for revenge. Curtis breaks in with his fist and hits me in the eye. It hurts for real.

"Get out of the room! Stop it!" What's your problem?" I am screaming and crazy. I reach for the hot curling iron and hold it like a weapon. I am going to put an end to this. I'm going to be the heroine! Curtis and Lee both run towards me; they are determined to win. I don't know which one to blame for the burn across my cheekbone from ear to lip, but once it happens the scene is over. The three of them stand there; Curtis, Lee and Audrey, eyes wide and mouths slack jaw—looking at my face like I'm about to get us all in big trouble.

Lee and Curtis pull the bed away from the door and leave. Audrey and I sit on the floor and look in the mirror— like we were five minutes ago before the boys barged in.

Now there is a burn on my face below my cheekbone. It's perfectly placed, looks intentional, like makeup. A bruise is forming on my eye—redness all around, but a deeper purple starting to seep up from below. I stare at these marks on my face and I don't hate them. I look at them like battle scars, not that I deserve them, but I've earned them.

How am I going to hide this from my parents? I'm not supposed to be in anybody's house without an adult around. I'm not supposed to be kissing boys. If I tell on Curtis and Lee for smoking pot, my parents will assume Audrey and I were smoking too. They might also figure out that it's Terry's pot, or think that he is a bad parent to have such a mean son. I can't lose Audrey; she is my only friend. I should have protected her. Everyone is going to blame me for everything. Somehow, I should have been in control of the mood of the house.

Audrey and I don't talk much about it. We look at ourselves in the mirror and put makeup on like we always do. I think I look a little more "streetwise" and wonder if that look will fade from my eyes as the bruise does. Eventually we go into the kitchen. Curtis and Lee are standing by the stove; they have a pack of cigarettes. Curtis takes one, lights it over the fire on the stove and hands it to me; a peace pipe. I've never smoked before in my life and as I take a hit I begin to cough violently. It tastes like shit, but determined to learn how, I don't put the cigarette down. As I bring the cigarette up to my lips again there's pounding on the kitchen window; it's my brother. He's pointing and screaming something about telling on me and he takes off running up the street. Curtis looks at me and asks "Is he really going to tell?"

"Oh yeah, Mr. Perfect is definitely going to tell on me."

Walking up the hill to our house, I wonder if the black eye and burn across my cheek is going to get me off the hook for smoking. My dad is busy working and doesn't notice my face at all. Something monumental has happened to me and I feel a little disappointed that it goes unnoticed. Late at night my mom comes home from work and eventually looks at me. When she asks what happened, my dad is prompted to notice and says, "Yeah, I was gonna ask you about that."

"Me, Audrey and a bunch of other kids were doing gymnastics on her lawn. I was at the bottom of the human pyramid we were building and I took a knee to my eye."

"Is that a burn on your face?"

"I was feathering my hair, and burned myself with the curling iron."

"You were in Audrey's house when her dad wasn't home using the curling iron?"

"No, the burn happened before her dad left for softball practice." I can't believe she cares more about her rules than the burn on my face. I want to tell her what really happened so she can feel sorry for me or comfort me—maybe even protect me—but I will only get in trouble for breaking the rules. Everything is my fault.

"You know you aren't allowed in their house if their dad isn't home."

"Yeah Mom, I know."

5 ● FREE TO JUMP SHIP

1979 ▪Twelve years old

There is a pile of wood below me. It's not stacked neatly like a lumberyard, but pieces of different lengths—scraps—thrown into a corner of the property that will eventually be our driveway. There is jagged metal in the pile and boards with nails sticking out.

I'm not sure what brought me to the roof's edge on this day, wanting to hide, wanting to jump. Those statements don't really play into this. I _want_ to _need_ to hide. In reality my dad is lying on the couch asleep. I've been home from school for two hours and he hasn't gotten up.

My mom won't be home from work 'til long after dark- it's been that way since she sat me down sometime last year and retired from motherhood.

"Things are going to be changing around here and you aren't going to like it. I can't take care of each of you and still take care of the family as a whole. From now on you will have to take care of yourself—cooking, shopping, and cleaning. I am going to be gone long hours trying to make money to complete the construction of this house and keep this family afloat."

That was it. One conversation and there were no more warm chocolate chip cookies after school, no more Saturdays at the movie theater sharing a bucket of popcorn.

It's not that I want to jump, there is some force inside me compelling me and I'm trying my hardest to resist the urges. But the impulses are winning today, because I've passed my dad on the couch, walked up the stairs, closed two doors behind me and climbed up and out of the window to get to this spot where I'm hovering over the edge of the roof and telling myself NOT to do it.

I'm supposed to be smarter than this.

I don't have an urge to die; but I don't have the will to live. I'm not trying to punish anyone, I can't get away from the feeling that it would be a favor, not a punishment, to relieve them of me. Having the option of falling to my death helps my mind to rest and get away from the grief.

It's hard to escape the sadness, it's a physical feeling that starts in my chest and fills it heavy. This must be what it feels like to drown – except that there is no death or relief at the end. I keep filling up, like I'm underwater and every movement I make is labored. The effort becomes harder with every move. I want to give up, give in. I know why they call it "Drowning in sorrow". Funny how diving off a roof could cure me from drowning. The idea of jumping off relieves the pressure from my chest so I can breathe easier.

"Why are you sad?"

They badger me with their questions. I can feel the physical sadness long before I can ever determine the *why*. Maybe there isn't a reason why? Maybe everyone's life sucks—but if you have a heart that fills up and gets heavy then you are someone like me who gets a sad, heavy heart. Maybe I could learn to have a hard heart, or a cold heart – then the sadness won't creep in. That must be how people become cruel. But I'm not hard, I feel everything getting absorbed – all the emotion around me. What I can't feel is touch—human contact—that sensation can't get in at all. If someone wanted to reach out to me, I wouldn't feel them, couldn't feel them. Maybe I don't want to feel them reach out. Maybe I would rather sink in my sadness than accept them as a life preserver.

We take threats of suicide seriously here Karen. We can't let you out of TLC until we can believe you won't hurt yourself. —Staff

I was telling you about the past, writing just like you wanted. I was not threatening to commit suicide. What the fuck do you want me to do?

That is a zero for language, you were already warned. —Staff

6 ● LYING UP TO EXPECTATIONS

1980 ▪Thirteen years old

I'm lying in his bed, staring at the ceiling. He's on top, trying to stick his dick in me. First it's poking my legs, then the bone below my pubic hair. Finally he pushes it in where it counts. Everyone says I will remember this moment forever. Brad's red hair and freckles, his face pink and twisted and dripping with sweat – he looks like the devil. The thought running through my head is "I wonder what Gina will say when I tell her I lost my virginity."

A couple months ago, Debbie, Gina and I talked about being virgins. We make a pact to tell each other who does it first. I know they thought it would be me – because I flirt, because I'm "boy crazy". When Debbie did it first, Gina and I were surprised. Debbie and Hector are in love. Besides he's almost 18 so I'm sure he's done it before.

I don't love Brad – I'm here under him now because he lets me ride his moped and take it home at night. I'm here because I'm tired of saying no to him and every other guy that isn't happy to simply kiss; they push and pressure for sex until they leave frustrated. Why not give in? Everyone is expecting me to do it. Kids at school have been calling me a slut long before I ever kissed a boy my own age. I'm laying here now in acquiescence of everyone's expectations.

There's no bright flash of searing pain like I have read about. The whole thing is over pretty quickly. I put my hand between my legs and there is no blood – only a gooey mess like egg whites – it smells a bit like pancake mix.

"Can I have a towel?"

"Yeah, hang on, I'll be right back."

Brad gets up, quick to leave the room but not so quick to return. I lay thinking—"Is that it?" All the delicious kissing and caressing

23

and grinding on one another is a hundred times better than the three minutes of having the devil grimace and grunt as he pushes inside me. It's okay with me if I never have to do that again. It would be nice if now that Brad fucked me he would claim me as his girlfriend, but I doubt it.

When Brad returns he has a glass of water in his hand and tosses a towel at me. He sits on the edge of the bed and stares off in any direction but mine.

"I should get you home soon," he says.

"Can I ride your moped home and bring it back tomorrow?"

"No, I need my moped."

"Oh."

I wipe his mess from between my legs and pull my panties up from around my ankles. He never even slowly and romantically undressed me.

"You ready to go?"

When I get home my mom is awake and upstairs. I've heard it said that "Once a girl turns into a woman" it shows. I hope my mom can't tell I've changed.

She looks at me like I'm still a child in her eyes.

7 ● CHANGES

1981 ▪Thirteen and a half years old

     I'm tired of the way everybody sees me. In the car one day my mom asks me how I would like people to describe me. It bugs me when she tries to have these deep talks with me, but I spend a lot of time later thinking about this to try to answer the question for myself.

     "She's the most honest person I know."

     "She's the nicest person I know."

     "She's so much fun to be around."

     These are the things I wish people would say about me, If I'm honest with myself, this is probably not what people are saying.

     "She's boy crazy." "She's wild." "She's moody." That's probably what people would say. Maybe they would call me pretty, like it's something I've achieved or worked towards. I'm not saying I don't want to be pretty, I'm saying being pretty isn't a big accomplishment.

     I like the way the punk rockers look, because they're not trying to please everybody. I like the music for the same reason. The music is fast and aggressive, it fits with how I'm feeling. I think about it for a long time, and decide I want to cut my hair short. I want to look different, I want to look tough, I want to look grown-up. I want to be in control of how others perceive me.

     I sit in the salon chair watching strands of hair five inches and longer falling to the floor—this seems more monumental to me than the night six months ago when I paid for my curiosity with my virginity.

So you gave your virginity to a boy you didn't love, and cutting off your hair to "become

25

punk" is more important? We would like to learn more of your friends, other "punks" you were spending time with.

Tomorrow morning you will have breakfast in the cafeteria with the other girls, and then attend school. —Staff

8 ● REALITY REDUCED

JUNE 1982 ▪**Fourteen years old**   **Aurora, Colorado**

I've been lonesome for company and afraid of everything here, I feel excited on my first day to leave T.L.C.

Entering the cafeteria for the first time, I am shocked at how many girls there are. There are over 100 young prisoners in here and maybe 25 staff. Everything in here is green, from the overhead fluorescent lights, the honeydew green walls, to the pale pistachio tiles on the floor. These colors symbolize inexperience and are probably chosen to remind us we've been plucked before ripening from the tree of life.

One table in the back seats adults only, like royalty. They sit with their eyes on us but not bothered by us. All of their faces are unfamiliar to me. In the center there are eight tables side-by-side with fifteen girls and one adult posted at each table. The crown jewel on display at the front of the room is the T.L.C. table, the outcasts among the misfits—two adults and three girls. Girls whisper as they survey me, but I can't decipher the specifics. Avoiding eye contact, my food is a welcome distraction. I finish everything on my tray for the first time since being abandoned here. It's not that the food tastes any better than when I was alone in the room, but knowing the food is divided among a hundred other girls, it seems imperative that I eat. I think about chickens pecking each other to death when kept in close quarters.

The hum of conversation in the room massages my ears. Girls at the big cottage tables are engaged in conversations that seem friendly, sisterly. Some of them are even happily talking with their captors. It's not quite a Norman Rockwell picture of family, but I didn't come from that anyway. It certainly looks less lonely than T.L.C.

Our time in the cafeteria is interrupted by that bell that has previously only marked time passing for me in solitude. Now the bell herds the girls to school in a calm, orderly fashion. The halls are hollow sounding, like a hospital. No, worse than a hospital. In a hospital there is the hustle of people trying to WORK to make things better. Here, everyone moves in slow motion, almost a superficial attempt at life, rather than active participants. Every movement seems exaggerated because there is barely any movement at all.

New doors I didn't even know existed open up and I'm led into what looks like a movie set for a standard high school. Everything is reduced; not shrunken down, but less-than. Halls are three people wide instead of six. Classrooms have ten desks, not thirty. Chalkboards are half the size of any I've ever seen. T.L.C. staff escorts me to a mini school office and I sit in one of two chairs where normally there would be five or six. When one adult enters the room, my chaperone leaves. The changing of the guard.

The principal's office is almost normal in size. The windows have the wire diamonds running through them but here the outside bars are missing. She watches me assessing, calculating my escape. I lunge and push her down; picking up her heavy wooden chair, I smash the window open and run, but only in my mind. If I knew where I was or had somewhere to go, I would; but running is pointless. I sit down in my chair, a lighter, cheaper version of hers. There is only one, no seat allotted for a parent here. I am on my own.

The principal starts, "You were a straight A student, volleyball team captain, student council president." Holding all my transcripts since first grade, even samples of my writing and drawings, she grips them in her hand like evidence, flipping, tapping, sorting, stacking. She's confident she knows everything about me. Then she says the same thing everyone has been saying about me lately; "Last semester you failed every class. What happened?"

"I am sure my parents told you what happened. I'm writing my version in my autobiography. Don't you read my journals too?

"I want to hear it from you," she says settling back in her chair like she is about to watch a movie.

I settle back too, and tell her, "I don't know what happened."

"You ran away and dropped out of school," she says, as if that explains all there is to know about me.

"Yup," I surrender. She holds my future in her hands with those papers, but not my past.

Back in T.L.C, my life is passing me by. Girls come in and out of the locked center after only a week; I've been locked up for almost two months. Whatever it is Staff wants me to do, to become, isn't happening to me. I'm told the same vague crap: "The change will come from the inside." "There are no magical answers."

Eating used to be a chore to me; now I overeat at every meal, leaving the cafeteria sick from accepting food any girl won't finish. Daily a new purple stretch mark appears, scars so much uglier than the three cigarette burns on my arm. I suppose a psychiatrist would speculate that I was eating my feelings, but eating is my only recreation. I am not allowed to smoke and I no longer skate ten miles a day.

It takes a full two months before I get to leave T.L.C. and move into a cottage. I've gained fifteen pounds, I'm looking healthy and corn-fed, is this the change they wanted? I think they just finally needed the space to lock another girl away.

I should leave instructions for her; gain weight, unclench your fists, wear your smile like a mask, draw hearts on glitter-covered paper and you will move up their ladder. That's the cure!

Someone should have told me what they wanted.

9 • TAMMY LEROUX

SEPTEMBER 1981 ▪Fourteen years old ▪Redondo Beach, California

Redondo Christian School isn't exactly populated with Christians. There are kids from tough areas whose parents scrape together enough money to try to give their kids a better life. Mainly it's full of kids who have been kicked out of other schools, whose parents can afford to put them in private school. I was taken out of my public junior high school because of some bullshit with my 8th grade teacher. My parents thought I was going to be kicked out, so my mom beat them to the punch.

Tammy Leroux is another one of these kids like me, she had trouble in school and her Mom paid to get her out. Tammy will never admit it, but I'm convinced she does poorly in school on purpose, to spite her mom. She is bright and manipulative and I believe it takes her a real effort to not get passing grades. Tammy Leroux was a child actress and keeping her grades low prevents her from working, which drives her mother crazy.

Photos of Tammy's brother line the hallway; shots of him surfing, soccer photos, him doing normal boy stuff. There's only one frame with a set of photos of Tammy in that hall; she's in pigtails on the set of "Little House on the Prairie". It's as if the only thing of importance Tammy's ever done is be an extra on that show. I guess that's why we get along so well—we both play supporting roles to the boys in our family. I still haven't figured out what great accomplishment I can achieve to get my picture up on the wall in my house. At least Tammy has her 15 minutes of fame.

Tammy's room is a landscape portrait of consumerism. Mountains of clothes and piles of cosmetics spring up like anthills, used once and then tossed to another pile. Her mom doesn't seem to mind the condition of her room, as long as Tammy herself looks well-kept and attractive. "Are you ready to go to diving practice?" Tammy's mom

31

yells from the bedroom doorway. "Yes, Mom, I told you I was ready!" Tammy says with more sass than my parents would allow. "Pull the sides of your suit up as high as possible, so your legs don't look so short" Tammy's mom advises. My mom has added extra Velcro to all my button up shirts so my training bra doesn't peek out.

Shopping with Tammy is a fascinating and terrifying adventure. We are in a drugstore looking around for a while and when we're done browsing she has makeup, perfume and jewelry in her hand basket. She steers us toward a gawky young male cashier, oozing with virginal, pubescent frustration and awkwardness. As I pay for my selections, she begins to chat and giggle with him, flirting and making him feel important. By the time he's done with my transaction, he is hypnotized by her face; her flawless skin, her beautiful ice blue eyes. He is so overwhelmed by how lucky he feels in that moment; how special he must be that a girl as beautiful as Tammy is talking to him, he can't see anything but her.

Hypnotized and stiff, he is no longer aware of why he's behind the counter. She never lets go of their eye contact as they chat, but I see her open her purse smoothly, undetectably slowly, stealthily take every item from her basket and place it quietly in her purse as she pulls out her wallet. She is a stealing assassin, a shoplifting ninja. I barely believe what I'm seeing myself, my eyes (and mouth) wide open. She sets the basket down on the ground and grabs a candy bar with one smooth motion— as if it was the only thing that was in her basket the whole time.

"Oh yes!" she squeals, "I can't wait to get something sweet inside me!"

Tammy is the best with innuendos. She touches his hand ever so gently, giving him a dollar for the candy bar. He forces himself to break his gaze and work the cash register, which gives her a split second to shoot me a bitchy look.

"Thank you." he says, "Please come back again real soon."

"I'll be back again; this is one of my favorite stores. *You* always have what I want!" The cashier has no idea what hit him. The blood won't be returning to his brain for at least a half hour.

"Oh my God what were you doing? You took all that shit right in front of him!" I say once out of the store.

"Don't look so obvious next time; you almost blew it for me," she says in a parental voice.

"Really." "*You* are going to chastise *me?*" This irony is not wasted on her.

"The best time to take things is when the cashiers are right in front of you; that way you can keep your eye on them." Sometimes the things she says are so classic Tammy, it's impossible to stay mad at her.

She has a dozen different techniques for shoplifting, and loves to demonstrate her skills in this area. At the bikini store she grabs several suits of similar color and pattern and then puts two suits on one hanger. She walks right up to the sales clerk smiling and holding eye contact as they count the hangers. Tammy offers them some compliment that makes them feel special as they hand her the little plastic card with a number indicating how many hangers she's taken into the room. She comes out with the same number of hangers, a swimsuit hanging on each one. Tammy also has the suit she wants under her clothes, where it won't be found if her bag is ever searched; it never is.

Because Tammy's face is simply a spellbinding work of art, her method of shoplifting hypnosis works on everyone. Grown men can't help but lust after her; they struggle to keep eye contact with Tammy and not undress her with their eyes. When I see men look at her I think of that Oingo Boingo song called "Little Girls" which is ironic because Tammy is on a campaign to find the singer of that band and fuck him— She says, "I'm certain he's just nasty enough for me."

Younger boys are so excited to be getting attention from her that they will stare and hang on every word. They are like puppies waiting for a treat; they can't look away for even a second. Women are mesmerized and will stare and try to figure out what her secret is; is it her eyes, her bone structure, her hair and makeup? Tammy has a wicked sense of humor and can have you laughing and at ease within seconds when she feels like it. Women want to be near her to catch her overflow, to learn something, or to avoid the risk of being on the wrong side of her ominous power.

Tammy steals stuff and gives it to me; the value to her is in getting, not having. For her it's the thrill of controlling people and getting things in that moment. For some reason I find this part of her stealing the most disturbing; why go through all the risk if you don't want the stuff? She gives me stuff I'll never use. I've never asked her to steal anything for me—if she gets caught I'll feel entirely responsible. Tammy doesn't feel responsible for much. I admire that about her as a protection against other people, yet fear it as her friend. I have no idea why Tammy is friends with me. I'm not sure what she is getting from it, but I know she is getting something.

10 • JACK

NOVEMBER 1981

I'm waiting for Tammy, in front of Redondo Christian School, staring down at my stupid white moccasins, wishing I had big clunky engineer boots with buckles. Everything about the way I look right now is cool except for my shoes. I've been secretly using "Sun In" and I like the way my hair has started to turn orange. It looks great against my black eyeliner, orange blush, and orange lipstick. I got orange beads and earrings and an orange and black striped skirt from Goodwill. I'm wearing a low-cut black V-neck T-shirt and black tights… and the stupid white moccasins.

A bunch of kids ride by on their bikes towards Redondo Union High School, which is three blocks from my school. One boy stands out the most in this group, riding on someone's handlebars dressed in full Punk Rock regalia; his faded dirty Levi's with writing all over them are tucked into his worn engineer boots. He has on a thin, stained white T-shirt with a button-up long sleeved shirt tied around his waist. The driver and pedaler of the bike looks only a little less punk but I'm sure most suburban moms would cross the street to avoid him as well.

In spite of my stupid shoes I yell out sarcastically, "Punk rock sucks!" to get their attention. The leader on the handlebars yells "Stop!" and that's exactly what they all do at his command. They stop right there and wait.

"You don't really mean that do you?" he says to me.

I look at him and shrug to say, "If I did, would I be dressed like this?" I wish I could disappear from my ankles down.

"Go up there," he commands. His followers do as they are told. His friends never say a word as he talks to me. It's as if he has control over them—like a spell; I feel myself falling under it too. He introduces

35

everyone but I really only get his name: Jack. Eventually someone in his posse speaks up to say they need to get to school or they'll be late. "I don't care if I'm late or not, go ahead and go, you pussies. Wait for me after school. I want a ride home." He orders them to say goodbye to me and they do.

Jack sits down next to me and pulls out a cigarette.

"I don't think that's a good idea, this is a Christian school, you know."

"I don't give a shit. They can't kick me out."

As he lights his cigarette I take a good look at him up close. This boy is absolutely beautiful. He has broad shoulders, dark olive skin, a couple earrings in his ear, wide masculine Italian nose, high cheekbones. He has a sarcastic, deviant smile that hints there's trouble coming. The sadness in his beautiful green eyes will absolve him of any trouble he causes. He looks seventeen or eighteen because he is so much bigger than I am, but he's only fifteen—a year older than me.

The first bell rings and it's time for me to go into school.

"Do you have a boyfriend?" Jack asks. When I tell him no, he says "What time do we meet for lunch?" I'm glad we both feel the connection.

"I'm not allowed off campus; this is a Christian school, it's different than yours."

"I can't wait all day to see you. What time do you have lunch, I'll come by to look at you from across the street."

He is serious.

We agree to meet by the playground fence. As the second bell rings and I'm walking away Jack yells after me. "Wait a minute! Don't I even get a handshake goodbye?" He holds out his hand, and I lay mine in his. He lifts it up to his lips and kisses it. The softest, sweetest kiss I've ever felt.

I tell Tammy everything before class begins. She is excited, but doubts he will show up at lunch. I don't have any doubts. It's impossible, but I think we're already in love. Concentrating on class is pointless; my mind is drawn only to him. I still feel the strength of his hand holding mine, feel the warmth and softness of his lips on the top of my hand. If his kiss on my hand can make me so distracted and overwhelmed with passion, what will his kiss on my lips do? Tammy asks me lots of questions by passing notes with her signature stick figure cartoons:

Are you sure it's only his big boots you find attractive?

My life is dramatically changed and everyone is behaving so normally, it makes me feel off balance. Can anyone else feel time passing so slowly today? It takes forever for lunchtime to come and the ten minutes we are required to stay in the cafeteria before we go out to the playground seems to take a year. I'm the first one out the door and annoyed when Tammy is next to me saying, "I thought you said he was going to meet you here?"

As the retort, "So did I," comes out of my mouth, I see him walking alone toward us. He looks regal, or like a warrior. I can't figure out exactly why my eyes are drawn to him, but I've noticed it's definitely not only me.

He sits on the sidewalk near me and I sit on the cinderblock wall on the other side of the chain-link fence and we talk.

"What were you into before Punk Rock?" I ask.

Jack sings loudly, arms reaching to the sky,…"and she's buying a stairway to heaven…."

I can't even imagine him with hippied-out long hair. He is the personification of punk rock now. Tammy keeps coming around talking for a bit and then leaving, then coming back again. She seems kind of smitten with him as well. I understand; he does seem to cast a spell.

"He is really cute, this whole day is like a movie, like a love story," Tammy says when we are back in class. I hope she doesn't try to steal him—she's prettier than me, but I met him first.

Jack is waiting when I get out of school and he walks me the two and a half miles home. I've never been walked home from school before; this day really is just like in the movies. He even carries my backpack. When I tell him we are a block from my house, he quickly kisses my cheek and says "See you tomorrow." Then Jack turns around and walks away.

The next morning I get to school extra early. I'm happy to see Jack sitting across the street waiting for me.

"I wish I had your phone number. I would have called you last night," I tell him.

"Yeah, I needed a night to break it off with my girl. But now

I'm all yours!" He smiles proudly.

 "So now you're mine?" I've never had someone give themselves to me like that before.

 "And you belong to me," he says.

 Of this we are both certain.

11 • LOVE

Jack waits for me at school every morning, by the fence every day for lunch, and walks me home after school. We talk on the phone at night for hours. On weekends, Tammy and I meet Jack and his friends at the mall. She is always so interested in spending time with us. I know every move she makes is in her self-interest. I wish Tammy would start to like one of Jack's friends; I'm nervous that she's gonna go for Jack at some point.

I'm excited because today both my parents will be home late; I have all afternoon to spend at Jack's house alone. On the way there, several kids we pass stop to talk, inviting him to do things. Each time he turns down an offer, I am proud that he's chosen me over them.

When we get to his house I'm excited without the usual accompanying anxiety. I'm not looking for an escape route. I am lost in his kisses, willing to go as far as he wants, not strategizing my next defense. Rubbing my hands along Jack's worn flannel shirt I feel his strength. Pushing his sleeves up to rub his skin, I feel ridges and rises— like one of those globes that show the height of the mountain by raising it up from the orb. I open my eyes and see scars up and down his arms. I know immediately what they are. I am drawn to them because they seem a solution to my ineffectual screaming into my pillow, hitting the walls and clenching my fists.

Noticing my eyes are open and looking at his arms, he pulls my chin up with his hand and kisses me, pulling his sleeves back down to his wrists.

"It's okay, Jack, I love every part of you."

I kiss his cheek, his neck, his chest. Then I pull his sleeve back up and kiss the scars on his arm. They are rough and crusty on my lips, I can feel where some of the cuts are new and the fresh blood has bubbled and dried – almost like a red zipper above his skin. I run my lips across them and one of the tiny balls of blood dislodges and sticks to my mouth. The cut is left with a fresh speck of blood and now it's like we are "blood brothers" forever. I know in this moment that I will someday cut myself. I am almost looking forward to it–knowing that there is a temporary solution to my problems, a relief in store when I feel overwhelmed by my parents telling me what to do or being mad at me for what I'm not.

"No one has ever done that before," he says.

"I love you. I understand. What does your mom say?"

"What can she say?"

When I see his scars, I feel the sweet pleasure and excitement of a secret friend, and I look forward to seeing them again, this time on my own turf, on my own arm, mapping out my pain, cutting it away.

I feel closer to him now, more intimate with him than if we had made love. Having sex with him seems like the next natural course of events. I'm not going to deny him, but I want to wait as long as possible, I want it to be romantic. Jack takes off his clothes, bold and beautiful. I admire his pride and lack of inhibition, desire his beautiful strong body next to mine. Surprisingly, he doesn't pull off my clothes immediately. He slides down my legs, slips off my moccasins and massages my feet through my tights. His hands slowly rub my legs, stopping long enough in between them to feel the heat as he reaches up to my waistband. Arching my back to make it easier for him to pull off my tights off, I am happy he doesn't try to immediately push his dick in me. I am shocked when he slithers back down and starts to suck on my toes.

"Oh my God! What are you doing?"

"Does it feel good?"

"Yes," I barely whisper, nodding my head.

"Then it doesn't matter what I'm doing. If you like the way it feels, let me do it."

I feel chills go up my body, and excitement between my legs even though he's not touching me there. What's in it for him to be sucking on my toes? Why does it feel so good? Maybe it's because he's trying to please me instead of immediately jumping on and trying to please himself. He slowly slides up my body, lifting my shirt up and over my head so we are finally lying chest to chest. It feels good to be this close to him. I've never felt so close to someone in my heart while they were trying to get inside my body. When he finally sticks it in, our bodies move together and it feels like we are making something – making love – instead of me giving in and giving something up. This is what I should've waited for when I lost my virginity. When we are done, we lay in bed together holding each other; for once I don't feel like getting up and taking a shower as soon as it's over.

There's a knock on the front door and Jack throws on his jeans to answer it. He comes back into the bedroom while I'm still getting dressed and tells me he has to leave the house for a minute and I need to stay here. He pulls on his boots, grabs a flannel and leaves in a hurry. I jump off the bed and rush to the living room window just in time to see Jack walk down the sidewalk with a man I've never seen before. I didn't get a look at his face, but his clothes were dirty, his hair looked greasy and he was probably twice as old as us. Why would Jack take off with this old dirty stranger? They turned the corner and I lost sight of them. Back in Jack's room, I light a cigarette and wait in his bed.

Jack comes back 20 minutes later wearing a brown fedora, a fresh pack of Marlboros in his pocket. He's holding a glass mayonnaise jar full of change in his arms.

"Who was that?" I ask, wishing he would volunteer the information.

"My dad."

"That was your dad?" I didn't mean to sound so surprised, but Jack never mentioned his dad and that man certainly didn't look like a dad.

"Yeah, he found this cool hat in the trash and wanted to give it to me. He gave me some smokes too, and this jar of money. He wanted to know if I knew where to score any acid." Jack spoke as if this was the most normal situation the world, and maybe to him it was.

"You've taken acid?" I've never met anyone who has taken acid before.

"Yeah, a bunch of times; it's fun."

"Have you ever taken acid with your dad?" I had to ask.

"No, that would be a guaranteed bad trip."

"The hat looks good on you."

"Yeah, I can make a trashcan hat look cool. Let's get out of here."

12 • MEET MOM AND DAD

On our three-week anniversary, Jack shows me a big surprise – he's tattooed my initials on his forearm. I am shocked at his love and devotion to me, touched by his incredible commitment.

"What are you going to do if we break up and you don't want to have this tattoo anymore?" I wonder.

"I'll change it to Kill Pigs," he says.

I know Jack loves me and understands me. I trust him more than anyone else I know. He makes it clear with his actions and words that he doesn't want me to look more punk or cut myself, but I know he will never withhold his love or affection if I do something he doesn't like. For the first time that I can recall I feel accepted. I have no reason to lie. He will love me no matter what.

At home, every mention of Jack is accidental. He is in all my thoughts and I am glowing in love. When Mom asks questions, I avoid details. In the past she would always say that I am "too young to have a boyfriend", but now she suggests I invite him over for dinner. I know this is less of an invitation than a potential interrogation. There is no possibility of my saying no to my mom.

Jack wears his nicest clothes: clean jeans, long sleeves and Vans tennis shoes. I've never seen him in anything but engineer boots. Even though he takes his earrings out you can still see the holes in his ear. You can't really clean the punk off of Jack. My parents don't try to hide their disapproval. My mom sees his tattoos through the thin white sleeve of his shirt. "What does that say?" she asks him, pointing to a spot on his arm.

"F. T. M.," Jack tells her.

"What does that stand for?"

"Fuck The Moon," he says and laughs a bit.

My parents are not laughing.

"Can I see?" my mom asks

Jack lifts up his shirt sleeve. All his scars from self-inflicted cuts and his other "do-it-yourself" tattoos pale in comparison to the fresh K.P. tattoo on his arm.

When my parents see it, they shoot dirty looks at me but they don't want to give Jack the pleasure of acknowledging that my initials are permanent on his arm. Even though my dad has a tattoo, they hate Jack's. I thought they would like the tattoo of my initials a little bit more than his others, but I can tell they hate it the most, because all conversation about his tattoos cease.

Eventually Jack gets to leave the worlds longest, most uncomfortable dinner and I am left with my mom and dad at the kitchen table.

"Is this what you want for yourself?" Dad asks.

"He is handsome and charming and funny and popular and nice to me! Why wouldn't I want that?" I argue.

"Do you think this is the best you can do? Is he high?" Mom tears him down.

"Of course he's not high! He was trying to make the best possible impression. He wore long sleeves so you wouldn't question him about his tattoos, but you did anyway! What do you mean 'Is this the best you can do?' He tattooed my initials on his body! He LOVES me!" The louder I talk, the less they can hear me.

"Well if he isn't high," Mom says, "I think he might be a little slow. He never holds his head fully erect, always tilted a little to one side or the other."

Nothing is ever good enough for my mom, ever. I decide right then and there to keep my relationship with Jack to myself as much as possible. Now it's "Us vs. Them".

Dark frustration and thick sadness shadow me to my room, consume me once I am alone. Relieved to let my defenses down, afraid I may not be able to summon anger over sadness to fight with them again. I think of the scars on Jack's arms, an alternative to pointlessly lashing out at my parents, only lashing out at myself. I can take control of if all with my own hands, with my own blade, on my own terms.

The first cut gave an icy pain as I slid the razorblade over my forearm. My skin opened up much easier than I imagined it would. I wonder what Jack uses to cut himself. Then the cut began to burn, not bad like a fire, almost gentle warmth, a good hurt. Staring at my arm like it's someone else's, feeling the pain as if someone else inflicted it, I wait for a pool of blood that never comes. It doesn't satisfy. Thick red blood forms tiny dots inside the cut. I'm determined to bleed more, cutting deeper the second time, but it's still not enough. I am waiting for the peace, the sweet release, but all I get is fear. How will I hide this from my parents? Am I going to have to hide this from Jack?

I get up and put the needle down on my Black Flag "Jealous Again" album. The cuts have pushed away the sadness and the music gives me energy. I spend the rest of my night locked in my room putting little plastic beads on fishing swivels and connecting them together to make bracelets. Over the last few months, I've collected cat collars and swivel bracelets, and stacked them up my arms. These items are fodder for my parents' constant criticism of my appearance, but at least they will hide the cuts.

No one says anything at home or school about the cuts. By afternoon I am thrilled and feel pride in knowing that I have something all my own, a secret. Jack meets me after school and I don't go out of my way to show him, but I certainly don't hide the cuts either. I like to pretend that I am not copying Jack, that the cuts have been there all along.

Jack's home life is the opposite of mine. His parents are divorced and his mom works 'til after five every day. Being in Jack's apartment alone is awesome. There's always a big pan of homemade lasagna and other snacks to eat. His bedroom is dark and looks like it has never been decorated. There are a few holes where he has lost his temper and hit the walls. Flyers from gigs are stapled and taped to the wall, but not in any kind of order. Jack says his mom hates it when he smokes in his room, but he does it anyway, setting the cigarettes upright on their filters to eventually burn out on the table next to his bed. There are burns on the carpet because this method isn't always effective. He's got a lot of great punk rock records to listen to and friends often stop by to visit. I feel grown up here, like a teenager instead of a kid.

Wasted Youth has an album that just came out called "Reagan's In". It's the soundtrack for a lot of our time in his room.

REAGAN'S IN

45

The best thing for us is his bed. I love that Jack knows so much more about sex than I do. I love the attention and stimulation and recreation. I had sex with two other guys before Jack and never really knew what all the fuss was about, but I do now. Jack's body is beautiful. He looks like a man, not a boy. He has sex like a man. He doesn't just want to jump on and fuck and jump off. He wants to rub up against me and kiss my neck, nibble on my ears and suck on my toes. Jack can keep his dick hard as long as I want, keeping it in me from behind, making me cum again and again. He talks dirty in my ear.

"One of these days I'm gonna bring Drew in here so you can have four hands all over your body at once. You would like that, wouldn't you? I see the way you look at him, he is kinda sexy, huh? We will give you so many orgasms that you'll beg us to stop so you don't pass out. If you let me eat you out, I will bring Drew over to eat you while you suck my dick."

"Ew. You know I don't like that. What's in it for you, anyway?"

"You suck my dick, what's the difference?"

"The difference is your dick is an extremity, I can see all of it. It's like a finger, easily cleaned, easily accessed. The skin is similar to the skin on your thigh or stomach. A pussy leads off into nowhere, you can't see it all. The skin is weird, different from any other part of my body. It's like a mouth. Labia, Clitoris, Uterus—there are so many words, so much unseen. Pussy is mysterious. Dick just is."

"It's time you get over it," he says, taking me by the hand and leading me into his mom's room.

It's the first time I've been in here. It's so much different than his room. There are big, bright windows with lacy curtains diffusing the light. The bedspread has flowers on it and lots of pillows, stacked up against a gold and cream colored swirling iron headboard. He tells me to lie down on her big soft queen bed. Everything is girly and romantic. This isn't gonna change anything, I think. He's still planning on stuffing his mouth in between my legs.

"Close your eyes and relax," he says as he lies on top of me. He is holding my hands sweetly as he kisses me, pulling them up above my head. He takes my fingers and guides them to the iron headboard and tells me to hold on. Then he starts to slide down my body like he always does, kissing and licking along the way. When his mouth starts to go past my belly button I grab him by the hair and pull him up. He's quickly in a sitting position on my hips and pressing my hands back to the headboard,

"Don't let go again," Jack says. "Keep your eyes closed".

His head is still out away from between my legs, so I'm still winning. My eyes are closed and I'm smiling when something cold wraps around my wrist and clicks. I know what that sound is immediately. I've heard that sound on T.V. I remember that sound from when my brother had a pair when I was six or seven. My hand is handcuffed to Jack's mom's bed, he's sliding down my body again and I reach down to pull his hair with my free hand.

He reaches down to the floor and grabs a shoelace and tells me, "I can either handcuff both your hands or tie your other hand up with the shoelace, but I'm going to stay here and eat your pussy 'til you like it. I promise it won't take long."

"Use the handcuffs." I lie still while he unlocks one cuff from the bed frame and wraps it around, clicking it onto my other wrist. I close my eyes tight in horror and excitement, like a roller coaster. That sound when you're going up, up, up, on a roller coaster, before the first big drop? That sound is a lot like the click, click, click, of handcuffs to me.

13 • DOMINIQUE

Jack and I are completely honest; there is no judgment. It's the most accepted I've ever felt in my life. The last few months with Jack have been a smorgasbord of sexual experiences.

When we fooled around with Drew I felt weird the whole time. If I enjoyed what Drew was doing, it might make Jack sad. If I acted indifferent around Drew, then his feelings would be hurt. My mind wouldn't let my body have fun.

Jack asks me how I feel about girls.

"When I was eight, I would take catnaps with my friend, cuddling under blankets and sucking on each other's nipples. Everything in books says it's normal experimentation and doesn't make me gay or bi-sexual. I want to experience being with a girl now. I think I'd still like it."

"No problem, I'd like that too."

"No, not for you. For me. I don't want you to be there, at least not at first."

He teases me about leaving him for a girl, but he's joking. Jack understands me and he isn't going to treat me any differently for telling him how I feel. It's what I love about him, about us. He was never weird about Drew, it was me who couldn't let go.

Only a few days after that conversation Jack tells me, "I met this chick at school and she wants to meet you. You're going to love her." He hands me a piece of notebook paper. There is a number above the name, Dominique.

"I don't know what to say to her." I am instantly nervous, awkward. "What did you tell her about me?"

"I told her you wanted to eat her," he says.

"God dammit, Jack! I can't talk to her now!"

"I'm teasing, I told her I had a cute girlfriend and you two should meet. Look, she wrote her number down for you. I don't even know how to spell her fucking name." He points to the writing and it's obviously not his.

Sexually with Jack, I am gaining confidence. Socially with Jack, it is easy to let him be in the spotlight and stay back in the shadows a bit. I'm not good at initiating conversation or reading people's faces. It even says so in the first psychiatric assessment of me at age 11: *Karen has problems reading social cues and assessing social situations.* I want to be more like Jack and do what pops into my head. My mom calls it impulsive. I think it would be great to be so comfortable being alive.

For four days, Jack questions me: "Did you call her yet? If you don't call her soon she's gonna think you don't want to talk to her."

"Okay, I'll call her tonight."

I keep Dominique's phone number in my pocket but I'm too nervous to call, unsure of what to say. I don't want to call her from my house, around my parents. I'm nervous enough without fear of my parents listening in. I hold the scrap of paper for days like a talisman for potential, knowing once I call, the spell will be broken. It will no longer be about possibilities; it will be "What Is". She will either want to meet me, which is horrifying; or she won't, which is horrible.

I've never felt excited to call a girl before, it's silly. Too much time has passed already. I'd better call from a phone booth. I grab the change that I stole out of my dad's sock drawer a few days before.

"Where are you going?" my mom demands.

"Down to Moonie's Liquor to buy some gum." I run the edge of the paper talisman under my fingernail while it's in my pocket.

"I have gum right here," she says, trying to keep me home.

"Do you have Tropical Fruit Bubble-Yum?" I know she doesn't, and I am not surprised when she gives me that look like I am up to something. What can she possibly suspect? "I'll be right back Mom, I'm only going to the corner and back."

"See you in a few minutes then," she says, giving me a time limit, but acting like it's a choice.

Walking to the liquor store, I pass small patches of grass surrounding telephone poles. Someone has taken to wrapping them in aluminum foil and wide red ribbon. Vertical twisted shrines that seem to multiply every year, shining monuments for all that is lacking. They are the universal totem for Christmas consumerism.

I use coins to buy gum, then walk across the street to the phone booth by the market, where I will see my parents before they see me.

"Hi, this is Karen. Is Dominique home?" My voice sounds like someone else to me, a quivering mousey voice.

"This is Dominique." She says her name to rhyme with "dome", instead of rhyming with "Tom". She sounds so exotic.

"Hi, Jack told me I should call you."

"Hi, I've been waiting for you to call. I thought everyone called you K. P., like the tattoo." She has the most cheerful voice, filled with enthusiasm, as if everything in her life is so awesome.

I can tell by the background giggles and laughter that her house is much different than mine. Her mom and sister are joking, listening to music. Dominique says they are listening to David Bowie. I've only ever heard the one song, *Changes,* because it was on the jukebox at my old junior high before I transferred over to Christian school. Dominique invites me to come over tomorrow after school.

"I can't do anything until the weekend," I apologize.

When I get back home I call Jack, proudly telling him I spoke to Dominique.

"I know, she already called me all excited. Two little lovebirds." He's happy for me.

Dominique and I talk on the phone every day after school. After a few days, she seems like an old friend, so I foolishly talk to her in front of my mom in the living room. My mom must sense my excitement because she starts to question me.

"Where did you meet her again? Does she go to your school? Why are you so excited to become friends with this girl?"

I can't begin to explain, but know better than to start. I can't tell my mom I won't judge people by the type of clothes they wear, or the music they listen to, or even by the type of genitals they have. Lots of boys are gross and a lot of girls are so beautiful. It's only been boys that have been interested in me, but it would be nice if a girl was. I'm too young to know what I want and too old not to figure it out. Now that I have had sex, every relationship will have sex as an expectation; I want to make the most of it. Curiosity fills my mind and colors my desires. What's wrong with trying everything? I got to have sex with two men at once, why not another girl? I want to know what another girl tastes like. Now that I know what it feels like to be handcuffed to a bed and surrender, made helpless—to be allowed to be shameless—I want more. I know better than to open the floodgates and tell my parents these desires. I only feel guilt about my thoughts when they are revealed to my parents. Perhaps that means there is something terribly wrong with me; maybe it means there is something wrong with them.

The lesson here is not to ever phone Dominique in front of my mom.

By the weekend, I learn a lot about Dominique. Our phone conversations are free and uninhibited. "My boyfriend Gideon's cum tasted like strawberries because he ate so many of them. I guess that's proof you are what you eat."

"What does Gideon think about you liking girls?"

"He doesn't mind, he's bi-sexual too."

I wonder if I am. I wonder if Jack is. Maybe everyone is bi-sexual but only some people know how to accept it.

I tell my parents I'm going to skate on the Strand on Saturday, but really, I am going to meet Dominique at Jack's house. When Saturday comes, it's raining and my mom won't let me go out. Dominique calls me from Jack's house and offers to walk the rest of the way to my house.

"Can my friend Dominique come over?" I ask my mom.

"You were planning on going to see her all along?"

"No Mom! I was planning on going skating, but it's raining and Dominique called and said she is bored at home and wants to come over. What's your problem?" I don't understand how my mom constantly knows something is "wrong" when I haven't even done anything wrong... yet.

Excitement fills me as I wait for Dominique. Is this how soldiers feel when they come home, about to see their sweethearts after so much time apart?

She arrives soaking wet; the yellow food coloring dying her short blonde hair drips onto her dress. She smells warm and soft but crisp and fresh—like baby powder and pine.

"I like the way you smell."

"Oh, Frangipani," she says.

I'm not sure if she is even speaking English.

Despite the mess from the rain she is more beautiful than Jack could have described. Her narrow eyes are framed by fake eyelashes that are balanced by her strong nose and light flawless skin. The lashes would look comical on anyone else, but look glamorous on her. She has beautiful straight teeth, all even in front, where mine have two big ones in the middle, like a rabbit.

I loan her a T-Shirt and she changes in the bathroom so I can put her dress in the dryer. I am surprised that my mom has not come downstairs to give Dominique the third degree. Once we are settled in my room, I'm not sure what to do. I wish I had a David Bowie album to put on; I decide on the new B-52's album called "Mesopotamia".

Dominique has this spunk that makes her hard to keep up with. The more time we spend together, the shyer I become. I am in awe of her and I suppose that has a lot to do with it. After about an hour of us listening to music and drawing, talking about bands we like and if we have any common friends, Dominique stands up and I'm afraid she is about to leave.

"So, you want to see my body?" she says with all the confidence in the world.

"Yeah," I say, excited. But I'm nervous, unsure of what I'm supposed to do at this point. Usually with boys, it's all about fighting them off while I figure out how far I want to go. It's about stopping something from happening, not making something happen.

Dominique strips off my T-Shirt she was wearing and dances around my room wearing nothing but her dark blue tights.

When I look at girls in magazines, I covet them. I want to be them or emulate them. They are not real. They are examples of what I *want* to be real. Dominique is real, and more beautiful than any of them. I want to reach out and touch her. I want to bravely stand up, hold her delicate hands and press my body against her breasts as we hug. Is it different, kissing someone the same size who is on the same level, our lips on the same plane? Why can't I will my body to move?

She doesn't dance to the music; the music moves her body. Her eyes are lidded in a trance. She seems completely unaware that I'm staring as she swerves and spins, her head swaying to the rhythm of the music. For one second her eyes open to meet mine and I can tell she wants a reaction from me. If I could get up and dance next to her, perhaps pull my shirt off —

No, I could NEVER do that. My body is like a boy's compared to hers. My chest can only be called a chest, perhaps titties. I've got nothing more than nipples on top of a bump of flesh. They protrude like a pigs snout, never curving round on the bottom like a boob.

Dominique's breasts are beautiful. I want to cup one, to feel its weight, hold it in my hand and feel its difference from mine. If I could just boldly reach out and touch her…

But I am still sitting.

I am sitting still.

Mesmerized.

Is love at first sight possible? I fell in love with Jack the moment I met him. I'm not talking about the physical lust and infatuation, but falling in love with a person's soul, their entire essence speaking to yours the moment you meet.

Her dance, her confidence has shown me so much about her. Dominique is brave, graceful and confident. She is in love with life and I believe I am falling in love with her. I don't know if I like girls, but I know I like THIS girl.

I am in love with the feminine things that I hear boys talking about but I have yet to see in myself. I feel myself loving her and then loving myself as a girl more, and that makes me love her more: infinity.

Awe fills me and makes me incapable of moving. I sit with my eyes wide open, feeling a cathartic, infinite love so empowering that I am strong and weak at the same time. I am stunned.

The song ends and she looks at me, disappointed that I haven't touched her. Can't she tell what I am feeling? Doesn't she know that she has won my heart forever? I sit here all shy and stupid and incapable of managing my emotions and physicality at the same time.

"Could you get my dress from the dryer?"

Fuck. My chance is blown and replaced with regret.

14 ● ONE OUT OF MANY

DECEMBER 31, 1981

There is an advertisement on KROQ, "This New Year's Eve, at the New Olympic Auditorium: The Blasters, Suburban Lawns, Saccharine Trust, FEAR, and Black Flag". Daily I ask my parents if I can go, but every time they say no.

"But everyone is going. Everyone! It's an all-ages show. You let me go to the Andy Gibb show when I won tickets and I was only 11. How is this any different?"

"I went with you to that Andy Gibb concert. I bought a ticket and sat behind you and your friend," my dad says.

"You let me go to the Stones' 'Start Me Up' tour." I'm trying every angle to convince them.

"That was a special circumstance because it was the Stones' last tour, and you were with your brother and cousin."

"Well then come with me to the gig, but there aren't assigned seats. You get a ticket to get in and everyone stands where they want."

He finally agrees. I don't even care if he's there, as long as I don't miss this show.

"If I clean out your van can we take some of my friends?"

"Fine, I'll be driving there anyway." I imagine him pretending to take us all, then holding us hostage and driving us to some yuppie approved event instead.

At seven o'clock the night of the show, the steps leading up to my house are lined with a half-dozen punk kids; my parents are in the living room looking out the window. I imagine the scene if Norman Rockwell painted it, Mom and Dad with their arms around each other surrounded in amber light in the window. Mom with an up-do, Dad with an argyle sweater, both of them with rosy cheeks, eyes wide, and mouths formed in an exaggerated "O" shape. The kids outside chewing bubblegum, hands in pockets, faces turned down towards the ground kicking at pebbles. There would have to be one guy with freckles and big ears but instead of hair parted straight down the middle he'd have a tall orange, spiked mohawk.

We all quickly work together to get my dad's tools out of his van and into the garage. While I'm impressed with our efficient teamwork, my dad pulls me off to the side to talk.

"I don't want these kids taking inventory of my tools."

"15-and 16-year olds aren't interested in Skill-Saws and hammers"

"This is how people get robbed." he says.

Fucking idiot. All we want is a ride to the gig.

Riding to the show, I sit in the passenger seat; the other kids sit on the floor in back. Talking with my dad isn't really an option; he basically accused everyone of being thieves, so what's the point? I want to sit in back and talk to Jack, Dave and Brenda. I don't know the other kids in the van. I want to make everyone in the van comfortable with each other, and wish desperately I was comfortable with myself.

As we pull into the parking lot of the Olympic auditorium, my dad instructs our group to meet at the van after the show. He reminds me that we've been here before to see a boxing match, but I don't remember the building. I do remember the boxing match—hundreds of people sitting together, watching two men bludgeon each other. Sometimes people got so excited they jumped to their feet and started screaming towards the boxing ring as if they were the ones fighting. Watching the fight made me feel dirty and evil, so I spent most of the time observing ugliness fall on the faces of the spectators instead. Looking around at people who paid to watch those men pummel each other was absolutely disgusting. The sick feeling in the pit of my stomach makes the memory stick with me. We were Romans watching prisoners forced to battle lions.

It is hard for me to imagine that we are in the same building. In this new scene, we are not the Romans. This is more like a scene in the movie *Close Encounters*. I feel like the main character coming up over the hill and seeing hundreds of people in a hazy, dreamlike, silhouette. Finally aware this other world does, in fact, exist. There is a club full of us! Realizing that I am only one out of many, that there are hundreds, maybe thousands just like me. I am involved in something so much bigger than me, something so much more important than the few in the South Bay. If my parents wouldn't resist me, I could be part of a bigger club and belong to something special. I am comforted by the thought that I am not alone.

The Olympic is a huge, dimly lit oval. There are empty stadium seats encircling the floor below. Beautiful people walk around or stand in front of the stage. Spiked and colored hair, engineer boots, chains, T-shirts with drawings and statements across the chests. I feel like I belong, or at least like I want to belong.

I need to belong to this group as much as possible.

My dad follows me like a shadow. Every time I turn around he's there, looking deep into my eyes and trying to read my face to see if I'm wasted or something. The Suburban Lawns and the Blasters play their entire set, a couple of hours, before he finally settles down in a seat with a bird's eye view of most of the stadium.

"Is this what you like?" he asks me as Saccharine Trust starts to play.

"Yes!" I tell him, "I love it all."

My dad looks lost and lonely sitting there in one of the stadium seats by himself. He should have brought someone to sit with. I feel compelled to keep him company but I don't want to baby-sit my dad at a punk rock show and I don't want him babysitting me.

"Dad, I'm gonna go walk around for a while." I force myself to break away from my guilt. It's my first punk gig, I can't really be expected to worry about his comfort.

"Come back and check in with me every half hour or so."

"Sure thing, Dad."

As I walk away from him, I try to imagine what other people are thinking. Some old guy with curly hair and a mustache sitting alone. Does he look like he's into the music? Does he look like he's here to hit on young girls? To me he looks like my dad being awkward and butting into my business.

Jack is hanging out with a bunch of kids I've never seen before. I am in awe of his popularity, insecure because there is so much about him I don't know. I can't see my dad from here so I grab Jack's cigarette and take a few hits. We walk around together for a while. Jack's pretty wasted but he doesn't have to check in with my dad every 30 minutes so it shouldn't be a problem.

Saccharine Trust sounds like crazy punk rock jazz. The singer is a poet and looks "normal" with his button down dress shirt and curly hair, more like my dad than the kids in the audience. When the song starts he wags his arms above his head and crouches down on one knee as if he is pleading with us to listen. Every word is important to him, he is earnest and urgent.

As Saccharine Trust finishes up their set, I go back and check on my dad again. I want to make sure he sees me now, so he might sit still and not follow me around when FEAR starts to play. When I get back to where he is sitting, he has a beer in his hand and seems more relaxed. At least part of the time he wasn't watching me, the line for beer is long. He didn't say anything about me smoking.

"I'll be back to see you after the next band."

He nods and looks disappointed that I am happy here and want to leave his side.

"Boo! Boo!" starts to fill the arena. "Fuck you! Eat my fuck!" The crowd erupts into a chorus of boos and shouts as FEAR takes the stage. Some people even spit at the band.

"Fuck off!" Lee Ving, the lead singer, yells back to the crowd. "Hey listen, I've got a joke for you all. How does a punk chick know when she's pregnant? When she pulls out her tampon and it's half eaten."

As the laughter erupts, I know this band is not going to win my dad over.

Several slam pits start as momentum builds. The main pit is close to the stage, allowing people to dive off it. Second and third groups forming in other areas are slightly less intense because they aren't pressed up against the stage, allowing people to easily step out of them.

Watching the bands, I'm drawn in closer and closer. The energy is infectious, the music empowering. I feel awake and alive. I feel high. A lot of the kids are drunk; anyone can get a beer here if you have money. I don't want to be drunk around my dad. I want to take in the whole scene without anything blurring my vision or hazing my mind.

Standing around the pit, bodies bounce off of me and I thrust them back in. Having free reign to push and shove is a great feeling. So many times in life I've felt assaulted and now I have a chance to push back without fear of retaliation. The more I watch, the more I want to go in. I want to slam, I want to be a bigger part of the energy and action. I feel like in order to be a full-fledged punk I need to go in, kind of like an initiation. I keep looking over my shoulder to see if my dad is watching me; he would be mad. There aren't a lot of girls slamming. I think Jack would be annoyed if he saw me in the pit, it's mainly guys. The few girls that are in there look tough and like they're having fun. This isn't like sitting around looking down on a boxing match. I'm crammed right next to the action, sweating with people, bouncing off of them, pushing into them. I get knocked into a person behind me, then that person thrusts me forward. I am riding a wave in this ocean of people. It seems as if there is no division between audience and performers. We are all in this together; the energy is reciprocal.

Walking back to where my dad waits, he shakes his head back and forth like he's disgusted by the whole thing.

"Be careful over there, it looks like a big fight," he warns me.

"It's not a fight, Dad. They're slam dancing, and they're all having fun, I swear." I know he can't comprehend it. "It's called a pit and there's one over there and over there and over there." I point to the different areas where the kids swarm around in circles, knees kicking high, hands clenched into fists and elbows coming up at their sides.

"Well, stay out of there. I don't want you going in there," he demands.

I'm mad at myself for coming over to him. My whole reason was to check out his point of view so I can go into the pit where he can't see me. Now I'm going to have to blatantly defy him and hope I don't get caught.

Walking far enough away from my dad that I can't see him anymore, I've lost track of Jack. FEAR is done playing and Black Flag starts. I know most of their songs. This is the last band of the night and my energy is at its peak. Stepping into the pit, I start bouncing around, surprised by how little contact I have with people once I am in the thick of it. I am bumped by elbows and my feet get stepped on, but it isn't like getting your ass kicked. As soon as I settle into a rhythm, I fall to the ground. Looking up, all I see is a big punk coming towards me, wearing jeans and boots, his flannel shirt flying like a flag from his waist. Certain I will be crushed, I instinctively curl inward. Suddenly, hands come in under my armpits and lift me to my feet, we nod to each other and then I'm back in the pit again.

The last song Black Flag played is *Six-Pack*, a song that actually got some airplay on the radio. It feels like the entire crowd breaks into chaotic motion, like a giant swarm of bees. The song lasts less than two minutes, and then it's over.

I can't find my dad in his seat, or anyone else I know, so I head towards the exit door. The parking lot is lit with floodlights and is bright as day, a stark change from the massive dark arena. I stand in place trying to remember where the van is. The smell of cigarettes and beer rises in the steam from sweaty kids walking past me. The excitement and energy are similar to what I've always seen in my brother and his teammates after winning a football game, but I've never felt it myself. In this situation there are no losers. WE have all won this battle. We are warriors that have defeated the lion and leave the arena feeling invincible.

Approaching the van, I can see my dad scanning the crowd for me. Jack is against the back bumper and doesn't look drunk anymore, but there's a friend huddled on each side of him as if something is wrong.

"Where have you been?" My dad starts in on me. One of the kids that rode with us throws up behind the car next to us. "I have to drive a bunch of wasted punks?"

"I'm not wasted dad, and you don't know anything. You thought they were going to steal your tools too."

"Can I sit by the window in the front seat? I might be sick again," the kid who vomited asks. My dad looks at me as if I've done something wrong.

Honestly, I'm not positive this kid came to the show with us, but if he sits in front, I get to sit in back with Jack.

Once we leave the parking lot and get on the freeway, Jack lays his head in my lap and I stroke his hair. His hair is flat, the egg whites he used to spike it before the show flake onto his inside-out sweatshirt. His skin is cold but wet with sweat. I put my hand on his chest and his heart isn't really beating as much as it is vibrating, like it's going too fast to keep a beat, like hummingbird wings.

"What's wrong with him?" I whisper to Dave, Jack's buddy.

"He took 16 black beauties."

"What's that?" I ask, pretty sure its speed pills, but wanting to make sure.

"Speed," Dave says offhand, like everyone knows and takes the stuff. "But a normal person would take one or two."

Jack looks gray and weak; I bend over and kiss his damp face.

The distance between the front seat and the back of the van has grown. While my dad is probably preparing a lecture about this being the last gig I ever attend, I am praying that Jack can fight for his life.

"Please let us take you to the hospital," I whisper in Jack's ear. We are teenagers, so much more afraid of our parents than we are of death. Is this what death smells like? Sweat, smoke and vomit in the back of a Dodge van. I smell beer coming out of Jack's pores. The smell of beer and FEAR.

Normally, I would be more concerned with my dad seeing Jack's friends wasted in the back of the van. But I'm so worried about the imminent threat of Jack's death, nothing else matters. How many weeks restriction would I get if my boyfriend dies in my dad's van? I pet Jack's face and stroke his hair, trying to act more affectionate than afraid.

"We can take everybody home," I whisper in his ear again. "I can have my dad leave you near South Bay Hospital. I'll say you are staying at a friend's house and you can walk in from there." I do my best to devise a plan to help him.

"Don't worry, I promise I won't die," Jack says, pulling my head down towards his and kissing me. It no longer matters to me if my dad sees us kissing, if it's the last kiss I'm ever going to get from Jack.

"How can you promise that? How many black beauties have you taken at one time in the past?"

"Five, so this should be three times the fun". He looks small and frail to me now, so much more like a kid than a man.

I don't want to leave Jack when we drop him off at his house. His wide eyes are distant and alone. He looks lost. Someone needs to stay with him. We should've had Dave stay, but everyone had to get home to their parents. Terrified that Jack won't survive the night, I leave what might be our last kiss on my true love's lips. I should be too young to know what bittersweet feels like.

With my sinking heart I get in the van. It's only us two now, and we don't know what to say to each other. Maybe we are afraid once we start, we won't stop yelling. The ten minute ride on the empty streets from Jack's house to ours is dead quiet. Pulling up to our house, I see that my mom is waiting, sitting at our kitchen table.

We take our places at the kitchen table and my dad tells my mom that the show was horrible.

"It's violent and profane! Everyone was wasted. She is not to go back to another gig."

"I thought it was fantastic. It doesn't have to be violent, you don't need to go into the pit and even if you're in there you don't get hurt." I try to stay calm and state my case clearly.

"What's a pit?" Mom asks.

I can't believe I am even talking with them. None of this matters! Jack may die tonight.

It's after 3 a.m. before I get to be alone in my room.

Lying on my bed I am exhausted, nervous, and desperate to know how Jack is.

Somehow between anxiety and fits of sleep, 7:30 comes and I can't wait any longer. I call Jack's house and he answers right away.

"I've been up all night and I am lonely," he says, sounding tired but antsy.

"I'll try to find a way to come and see you today." I'm not sure what kind of trouble I'm in from last night yet. My dad was too pissed and tired to issue out punishments when we got home.

"So, how did your dad like the show?" Jack asks sarcastically.

"My dad is more determined than ever to keep me away from anything to do with punk rock."

"Guess that's the last time he'll give us a ride to a gig," Jack laughs.

15 • BROKEN

Jack and I are outside on my driveway, embracing in the dark, against my dad's van. The same van Jack almost died in only two weeks ago. My dad is three cans into his post-work drinking, dozing on the couch with the television on. He won't bother to get up and check, he assumes I'm in my room.

Mom's at work but she could drive up any minute. Jack and I get nervous every time headlights come around the corner. If my dad did look out the living room window for us, we are out of his view. He'd have to open the front door to see us; by then Jack would have time to run and hide. When my mom does drive down the street, Jack will run in the other direction. With this plan, we feel safe from attack on either side.

Hiding up against the van, we want to feel like we're alone on an island, when really we're in plain view of at least one of my neighbor's houses across the street. It's unlikely they'll come tell my parents I am making out, getting felt up in the driveway. I don't mind the idea of that nice, close Christian family watching me. Watching them out my window for the past four years has been like watching a sitcom based in the 1950s, so they've always held a distant fascination for me. One winter, they dug their own pool. Dirt came from their backyard one wheelbarrow at a time. The teenage boys got stronger and tanner, the youngest blonde daughter in her dress, serving lemonade. I remember my dad watching them toil and sweat from our kitchen table: "I bet by now they wish they rented a backhoe." By Easter, a big truck came and hauled the dirt pile away from their front yard. Then the cement truck came, the whole family still working together. By summer, I could hear them in their backyard, splashing and laughing.

Jack wants to fuck right here in the driveway, but I'm not into it. Maybe my body is 80% there, but my brain can't get me the other 20%.

"Listen Jack, we need to figure out what to do. I still haven't had my period."

"Well then, you're good to go." Jack says as he tries to unbutton my Levi's again.

"God dammit Jack I'm serious!" I've been trying to talk with him about this for weeks; Jack reassures me that I will start my period any day now.

"You never talk to me about this! I don't know what to do!" I shove his shoulders hard, pushing him away from me.

Jack pushes me back just as hard, knocking me into the van. "How the fuck am I supposed to do anything? Do you want me to reach up inside you and cut the umbilical cord with my fingernail?" I honestly don't know if that would work or not. I think he is just being mean.

Tears escape my eyes, but not before I see a different look in his. Jack looks irritated, finished with me, more trouble than I'm worth. He isn't mad, just done with me. Why am I such a crybaby these days? Maybe because everything sucks right now. My parents have kept a tight chokehold on me since the gig. I have had fewer opportunities to sneak away to see Jack. We certainly haven't had long days of hiding away in his room making love like we used to. I don't blame him for being sick of me, I am sure there are many other girls that are happy to have him, whose parents are far less controlling.

"I can't deal with your crying. I'll see you tomorrow," Jack says as he starts walking down the driveway.

"Fuck you Jack, you're such an asshole!" I yell at his back. He keeps walking. I don't want him to leave. I don't want to be alone. Catching up with him in the middle of the street, I wrap both my arms around him from behind.

"Don't go!"

I expect him to turn towards me and hold me gently, kiss my face and stroke my hair, tell me "It's okay, baby, we will work through this, everything's gonna be okay." But instead he pushes me off and then tosses me to the ground, flat down, in the middle of the street. He pulls his foot back and I twist just enough to protect my stomach as his boot connects with my ribs. The air pushes out of me as my eyes close tight; the eventual inhale stabs my sides like knives. I grab at my ribs and don't dare let go. Pain pulls my eyes wide open, but I can't find any emotion in his face. I see his eyes scanning me as his foot kicks again. Bile forced up burns my throat. I spit it out and search his face for answers, cues as to how I should respond. He looks like he always does, not a care in the world, not even mad really. I look past him to the

Christians' house, and then to my house; No one is rushing out to save me.

I'm curled in the fetal position. As I try to roll over onto my hands and knees, the pain in my side lays me flat out on the street. Jack comes to my rescue and helps me up. We wrap our arms around each other's waists and together we walk back to the side of my dad's van.

We're back safe on our island. I'm not crying now, needing to be strong; I want to protect my heart and my body from him. I need to detach from myself, pretend this just happened to someone else. I cross my arms, my right hand holding my ribs, my left hand holding my stomach the way a woman would if she was eight months pregnant. I stare at my feet. I don't want to look at Jack's face anymore, don't dare confirm he has no regret. Headlights come down the street, Jack ducks behind the front of the van but the lights continue past.

Jack walks around the van as he lights a cigarette; he takes a hit and hands it to me. I try to inhale but can't; I want to so badly. A big long drag off a cigarette sounds great right now, but every time I take a breath, I feel like I'm being stabbed.

"Here take it," handing it back to him, "I can't smoke, I can't breathe in."

"I should probably take off before your mom gets home," Jack says.

"Yeah, I need to go inside."

"I love you," Jack says, putting his hand under my chin and lifting so our eyes meet.

"I love you too Jack," I say as I close my eyes. I don't want to see his face.

Do I love him? In my mind, I have to answer yes, even though my heart and body hurt. I know I love him because even when he kicked me I still worried about us getting caught, I worried about someone seeing he'd done that. That's what love is, right? When you care about someone more than yourself.

"Can you sneak away from your parents after school tomorrow?" Jack asks, stroking my hair, kissing me all over my face. Why now? Why does he have to do all that stuff now? Why couldn't he do it when I ran out to him in the street, when I needed him to hold me? He doesn't seem sad or upset about the fight in the street. In fact, he is so cavalier, perhaps I shouldn't think it's a big deal. Maybe kicking me is not his fault. Perhaps his reflexes took over and he thought he was being attacked. It was a bad reaction, not an assault. He wasn't thinking. Tomorrow I will find him after school and everything will be fine.

My dad is asleep on the couch when I walk in the house and I'm relieved, I guess. He missed the whole show in the street. I'm certain if he looked out the window and saw Jack kick me, my dad wouldn't come to my defense, but I would be in trouble for sneaking out to see Jack. The relief that my dad is sleeping evolves into resentment.

I want to lie down and listen to sad music and cry for hours like when I was ten years old. Back then, I had no reason for the sadness that enveloped me and weighed heavy on my chest, compelling me to cry. Now I have a reason, but can't release the emotion. I will have too much explaining to do if my parents discover me.

Safely locked in the bathroom, in front of the mirror, I pull my shirt up and see the red circle where Jack's boot connected with my ribs. It'll probably be a real bruise soon; it's already starting to turn colors. No mark on my stomach, did I imagine the second kick? As I wash dirt and tears from my face I replay the incident in my mind and wonder, did he kick me because I'm pregnant, or because he thought I was attacking him from behind?

In fifth grade when Curtis hit me, I remember staring at myself in the mirror and seeing someone new. Here I am again, a completely new person. I don't look pregnant, at least I don't think so. My boobs are a tiny bit bigger, but they were supposed to get bigger anyways; after all, I'm fourteen and a half.

Digging through the medicine cabinet I find aspirin and pour four into my hand. Having never learned to swallow pills, I chew the bitter round tablets and gulp down water. I hope this will either stop the pain in my side or jumpstart my period. Something has to stop or start, it can't stay the same. I go to my room tired and broken, finding comfort in my bed.

Before my alarm ever goes off in the morning, pain wakes me from sleep. I walk slowly to the bathroom to look at my side. Stabbing jolts take my breath away as I pull my shirt up above my head. There's a black and blue bruise on my left side, my badge of betrayal.

After a shower I'm feeling better and become used to taking shallow breaths. When I go into the kitchen for toast to settle my morning nausea, I'm surprised to see both my parents at the table. It's so unusual to see them together that naturally I assume I'm in trouble.

"Good morning," my mom says. "How are you?" It sounds like an accusation to me. She may as well be saying, *"What are you hiding from me this morning?"*

"Do you think one of you could give me a ride this morning?"

"Do you need to stay home from school?" my dad asks.

God please don't make me stay home from school, where my parents can pop in and out all day to check on me. It's not like they would do it to care for me, just to make sure I didn't have Jack over. No matter what, I want to get out of the house.

"I'd just like a ride to school." I try to sound casual.

"I'll give you a ride, but you have to get yourself home." My dad doesn't want to be obligated to pick me up.

"Thank you." Now I know no one will be looking for me right after school.

As soon as I'm dropped off in front of Redondo Christian School, Rideaux walks up and asks why I am holding my side. A friend will notice something in 30 seconds that parents don't want to see all morning. Rideaux is a senior at the school. He is kind and helpful and hopeful, in spite of the fact that he describes himself as "ugly".

"Jack and I got in a fight last night," I tell him.

"You got in an argument with your boyfriend and he hit you? There is never a reason for a boy to hit a girl!" Rideaux says this like it's some kind of law; a universal knowledge that everyone but me has always had access to.

"Where is that guy?" Rideaux wants to protect me.

"He didn't mean to hurt me, I startled him from behind." I want to protect Jack.

"What were you fighting about?"

"Promise not to tell anyone?"

"You know you can talk to me," Rideaux says. I need to believe him so badly.

"Not anyone… ANYONE! No matter what." I try to look as stern as possible.

"I promise," Rideaux says in all seriousness.

"I think I might be pregnant, and Jack won't talk to me about it." The words seem to grow as they leave my mouth. Like one of those speech bubbles in a newspaper cartoon, one word hovers above; big and dark. **PREGNANT**. This is the first time I've said that word out loud to anyone but Jack. I wait for Rideaux to say something; judge me, chastise me, threaten to tell on me, but he patiently waits for me to continue.

"I want to have kids. Me and Jack will be together forever. We made this baby from love, why not start our future now? We could raise the baby the way we wished we had been."

"And what if your child is holding their side in pain someday?"

Rideaux's words leave us sitting in silence. They leave me feeling stupid and alone but I believe that was not Rideaux's intention.

All day in school I am distracted, my mind is somewhere much more important than anything these teachers can tell me. These assignments are silly, inconsequential, like asking Beethoven to play *Chopsticks*. My hatred for everyone grows, their lives are so simple, so little to think about. They giggle and talk about boys, recount last night's

T.V. shows. Their words swirl around my head and I want to turn them tangible—into a lasso and strangle them all. I'd do anything to be carefree, but I hate them all for being that way. I need a barrier, a way to demonstrate the profound difference between "them" and "me".

When school is over, I am surprised that word hasn't gotten around. In the future I must remember that boys are better at keeping secrets than girls, or so it appears. As I scan the sidewalk, hoping to see Jack, Rideaux comes up behind me and hands me a letter.

"I wrote you a note. I have to get on the bus to go home, so let's talk tomorrow."

I was left alone to read.

"I figure I can say more on paper. I do love you a lot so naturally I don't want to see you throw your life away by having a baby. A baby is NOT your answer to getting rid of loneliness. LOVE IS! A baby can't give you the kind of love you need at this point of your life. A baby ONLY cares whether it's fed, or changed or sleeps. It would be a responsibility you would regret later when you see that you can't go out as much, and especially when you see that guys kinda back off of girls who have kids. You just can't NOT believe in love because you've had a few bad experiences. That always happens. Someone out there is the perfect guy for you, but if you keep acting up you'll let him pass by. What I want for you, little sis, is a "taste of success."

I wipe my tears and stuff the letter into my backpack. Perhaps Rideaux knows more about me than I thought. Am I lonely? Am I acting up?

Jack isn't home when I get to his house, and I don't know where else to look for him. Skating home from there takes monumental effort; I swear the burden I am carrying slows me down.

16 • TRAIN IN VAIN

My parents are upstairs. I'm downstairs speaking in whispers on the phone with Jack. It's been a few days since he kicked me. The pain in my side is still there and so is the bruise. Jack's presence in my life has shrunk as the bruise has grown. He isn't around after school; I can't catch him at his house. This is the first conversation I've been able to have with him about "Everything."

"You're right, it's best if I wasn't pregnant, but I probably am. What are we going to do? We can't have this baby. You've been on plenty of drugs and I've smoked cigarettes. What am I going to do about my ribs? They are going to completely snap in half as my belly grows bigger."

"So get an abortion, you're not the first girl to need one. You act like I did this to you! You wanted to fuck, you wanted to have threesomes, I gave you everything you wanted."

Jack doesn't have any answers; he doesn't even acknowledge that he hurt my ribs. He doesn't have a car or money to get us an abortion. These problems are all mine in the end. Hanging up the phone, I cry into one of the pillows on the couch. Before my mom retired from motherhood, she made this pillow by hand, a needlepoint bird, framed in black satin, soft felt on the backside. Tears stain it and leave their mark. I don't care if my mom comes back to it later and sees my contribution to the family décor.

I need a plan, something to do besides cry. Tomorrow I'll have Jack ask his mom for help. She won't want her son to be in trouble so maybe she won't tell my parents. We need to take a step in some sort of direction tomorrow, no matter what.

My parents come into the living room and my dad is yelling, raging.

"We listened to your phone call and I can't believe what I'm hearing! You're pregnant and you want to have an abortion, with no concern for the life that is growing inside you? You're on drugs? Were you slam dancing with your baby inside you? You have no values!"

They are so angry, I know nothing will calm them down. It's as if my pregnancy is a personal assault on them as parents, their grand inconvenience rather than something I am going through personally. I don't know how to ask for help.

My dad continues his verbal assault while my mom just stands there. "I can't believe you've let this boy pass you around to all his friends and use you! Aren't you going to leave anything for your husband?"

What an idiot. His statement is wrong in so many ways, I don't even know what to think of it. Why is my dad even thinking about what I'm going to do with my husband? It's unlikely I will marry a man that would let me have a threesome or even a girlfriend. I don't feel bad for having sex, I feel bad for getting pregnant. I need to not be pregnant, I need birth control pills. I am in an impossible situation now, but that doesn't make me regret every experience I've had in the past.

Never have I seen such rage and disappointment in my parents before. They tell me how horrible I am, how immoral I am, I have no respect for my life or anyone else's.

"Have you even considered having the baby, or was your only thought to kill it?"

My mom shoots this loaded question at me. They hate Jack so much, yet all of a sudden they act like the greatest thing in the world would be for him and me to start a family.

"You guys are just now finding out about this, but I have been thinking about it for a while. I know that no matter who you ask, there are plenty of people who regret having abortions, but I've never heard of anyone regretting having their child." I look directly into my mom's eyes. "I need your help."

"I am not about to raise my grandchild, I'm hardly having a great time raising my daughter."

I don't blame them for not holding back. As they yell and list all my inadequacies, I hate myself as well. I dig my fingernails into my arm, forming little crescent moon shaped dents; the centers of some are red where I have pressed hard enough to break the skin. They yell; I grip and squeeze. I would prefer they physically hit me instead, they would tire sooner. As the berating continues, my arms numb to my attempts at distraction, so I claw at the skin on my face. I fantasize that the shock of watching seeping blood turn my tears red will make them stop yelling, but I am not bleeding enough. They never notice; they are blinded by rage. It takes over an hour of this shit before they are exhausted and I'm dismissed.

Running over the details of my phone call with Jack as I try to fall to sleep, I know I mentioned my ribs being hurt. Why didn't my parents ever mention that part of the information they had? I know they know he kicked me. They probably figure broken ribs are only the beginning of the penance I should serve.

The next morning my mom is at the kitchen table, phone to her ear, the big phone book in front of her. "My daughter needs to have an abortion," she says into the phone; disappointment and anger are at the root of her words, but sadness sneaks out and makes her voice crack. Is she about to cry? I have never seen my mother cry.

"You need to have a positive pregnancy test first," she says as she hangs up the phone. We will stop by Gina's house on the way to the doctor."

"What? Why do we need to stop by Gina's?" In the two years that we have been best friends, my mom has talked to Gina's parents maybe four times.

"Your sexual maturity has had a negative influence on Gina. I think it's only fair to Gina that you tell her what the end result of your promiscuity is." Her stare is cold and blank, cutting at my soul until self-preservation kicks in and averts my eyes.

No matter what I say to my mom, she cannot be convinced that it's a bad idea to tell Gina's extremely Catholic parents their daughter is no longer a virgin and that I am in the process of obtaining an abortion. During the ten minute car ride to Gina's house, I try to guess my mom's motives. I know she wants to embarrass and humiliate me, and solidify my guilt. She wants to warn Gina's parents about the incredibly horrible influence I have on their daughter.

Gina looks confused when she answers the door. I hope she can read from the horror in my wet red eyes that I would do anything to not be here right now, to NOT involve her in this.

"Karen has something to say," my mom starts, once we are all seated in their family room.

"I'm here to say I'm sorry for being involved in the punk scene. A lot of the kids we're hanging out with are bad influences and like to get into trouble. Gina might be better off finding some other friends." In that desperate, ashamed moment, I am sincere. Maybe I wouldn't be in this situation if I hadn't been hanging out with those kids. I look up at my mom and hope I've said enough to satisfy her.

"And…" my mom urges me to continue.

"And I have been having sex and want to warn Gina before anything horrible happens to her."

71

"What kind of things?" my mom won't let it rest. She has to make me say this to them, but she doesn't know Gina's parents like I do.

I stare down at the white linoleum floor with gray patterns. I always thought it was strange that their entire house had linoleum instead of carpet. Gina's mom, Geraldine, is frail and sick with lung problems, so she can't have carpet in the house. She only ever leaves the house to go to church. Last year we got in trouble for roller skating in the house. We were listening to Train in Vain by The Clash , skating around their pool table. We accidentally left stopper marks all over the floor and her parents made us scrub them off with Brillo pads.

♫ All the times
When we were close
I'll remember these things the most
I see all my dreams come tumbling down
I won't be happy without you around
So all alone I keep the wolves at bay
There is only one thing that I can say
Did you stand by me
No, not at all
Did you stand by me
No way ♫

"And because I was careless and made bad decisions, I'm pregnant and I have to have an abortion." I don't want to look up from the floor, I want to crawl under it.

Gina's confused; I never told her I was pregnant. She could be mad, she's obviously going to be in a lot of trouble with her parents. She could be worried about me, I honestly don't know how she feels about abortion, she's been raised Catholic. I was completely against abortion until I found myself pregnant at fourteen with what feels like broken ribs. I may be losing my best friend at this precise moment. Then I understood why we were there. My mom's motivation became clear to me; she was shredding the last safety net I might have had.

"No! You can't have an abortion. Please don't kill your baby!" Geraldine is hysterical. In the few years that Gina and I have been best friends her mom has never exerted this much energy. She's usually lying in bed, weak.

"You can have your baby and have her adopted. Gina and her brother were adopted, they were gifts from God to me!" Now she's standing up tall, her eyes are big, her face is red. It's like the Holy Spirit himself has re-animated her to save my soul, to save the life of my baby.

I've always wanted to have kids. It's one of the only things I've known from an early age. In the beginning, I was unable to even express my deep desire to have the baby because it was such a big secret. But now that my parents know, now that my mom's insisting everybody know, maybe the possibility of having the baby is an option. I wonder if Geraldine's antics will sway my mom. They're certainly swaying me. I can't possibly kill my baby. After all, this baby was created by me and Jack in love.

17 • FIXED

The ride to the doctor's office is quiet. Mom says nothing, leaving me alone with my thoughts. What about adoption? Is that something I could do, carry a baby for nine months and then give it to strangers? Would my parents let me keep it? What about abortion? My parents acted like I was preparing to commit murder, that I am going to burn in hell, but I don't even think my parents believe in hell.

The silence of the car is too big. I'd prefer her yelling at me, to being trapped in the car suffocating in silence. When we reach the doctor's office I follow my mom inside, but her silence is my only real companion. Once inside the waiting room, she adds my name to the list on the clipboard.

"Karen?" A nurse calls. She hands me a plastic cup with a lid on it. "Write your name on the cup and leave your urine sample over there," the nurse says, pointing to a narrow, paper towel lined shelf. Yellow circle and half-circle stains make a pattern on the towel. There are two other cups waiting for their answer.

It's been years since I've had to do this, but I remember being five or six and my mom holding the cup for me and being too embarrassed to pee. I didn't know how to tell her I could hold the cup myself or that I wanted her to leave me alone in the bathroom. I was crying out of embarrassment but my mom didn't understand why I had such an issue peeing into a cup. Now, at fourteen, I don't have any trouble holding my future in my hands and pissing in it. Leaving my cup of warm fluid in line with the others, I wish I could prolong these last few moments of not knowing for sure. I think the sliver of doubt is what is keeping the weight of the situation suspended above my head instead of crushing me.

The eyes of the other women in the waiting room are on me as

I take the empty seat next to my mom. They are all much older than me. We sit in silence, reading magazines or staring at our hands. Inside we are all pacing, and the energy comes out in our hands, feet and eyes. Next to me my mom is the picture of class and grace. She doesn't fidget, knees pressed together, ankles crossed and tucked slightly below her, off to one side. Her hands are in her lap with her fingers entwined, her chin is held high. Her constant state of composure is her defense against me. I wish I could develop that shell to protect me from the world.

"Karen, the doctor will see you now," the nurse says, and I follow her back behind the waiting room door. My mom trails after me.

"You can undress from the waist down, sit here, and cover yourself with this sheet. The doctor will be with you in a few minutes." The nurse turns her back and starts to walk out of the room. I look at my mom, terrified. Is she going to say something? I never agreed to this.

"I was not aware that Karen would be having an exam today. Can you explain to me why?" my mom asks the nurse.

"To see how far along she is."

"I see. Thank you." My mom dismisses her.

As the door closes behind the nurse my mom asks, "Do you want me to stay in the room during the examination?"

"What exactly are they going to do?"

"The problem is you've done everything backwards. You're supposed to have a doctor's exam before you have sex and then you're supposed to be married before you get pregnant. Now you're going to have to lay down on this table, so the doctor can come in and look between your legs. I'll leave you to get undressed, and I'll be back when the doctor is done." I guess the option for her to stay with me dissolved as her frustration with me grew.

The doctor steps in, shutting the door behind him. "Your pregnancy test is positive." He announces as if discussing the weather. Though he holds my paperwork in his hands, he stares down at me and asks, "How old are you?"

I won't talk to him. As long as he has his clothes on and I am naked under a paper sheet, there is nothing to say. I have got to keep something for myself—some bit of me that he can't touch and right now that is only my voice. He is more than three times my age. Is it even legal for him to do this, to be in a room with me when I'm almost naked? I am going to sit quiet and pretend the body under this thin cover isn't mine.

"Go ahead and lie down. Put your feet in the stirrups and scoot to the edge of the table."

I comply, making sure the sheet is covering as much of me as possible.

"Scoot down more, all the way to the edge" He turns on a bright light and aims it directly between my legs. I can feel the heat from the light bulb. I think of those old movies where a detective shines a bright light at the person he's interrogating. This seems totally unnecessary, just one more thing to make me uncomfortable. I am much more exposed in this room with the doctor than I've ever felt having sex. My mom waiting outside the door is the gun to my head necessary to ensure compliance. With closed eyes I silently repeat my new mantra—"This is what I need to do to NOT be pregnant."

He lifts the paper sheet up to my knees, so that it creates a barrier between us. I feel his gloved hand on me down there and then comes something cold inside me.

"You will hear a little click," he says, and then I feel myself opening like the hood of a car.

He grabs instruments from his table beside him and although I can feel him doing stuff down there, I don't know exactly what is going on. Moments later I feel the thing stop stretching me and hear it drop with a clink on his table. Just when I think that the humiliation is over, he stands up, crams two gooey fingers inside me and uses his other hand to press down on the space below my belly button. I gasp in shock and horror, then the pain in my ribs makes me hold my breath and I pinch my eyes tight to hold back tears.

"Do you plan to terminate or carry to term?"

"What?" I have no idea what he's saying. Why the hell is he talking to me while his hand is inside me?

"Are you planning on having this baby?" the doctor asks.

"No, I can't...." I have no words to continue. It is impossible to communicate with this man after suffering such humiliation. I bring my focus to the pain in my ribs instead of the gooeyness between my legs. I mentally repeat my mantra: "This is what I need to do to NOT be pregnant."

"Is that your mom outside the door?"

I nod my head.

"Do you want me to discuss your options with her present?" he asks as he pulls his fingers from my body.

"I guess so. She brought me here." I didn't know I had an option. After all, she's paying for this.

Turning off his warm interrogation light he says, "Okay, you can go ahead and scoot back and sit up. I'll call your mom in." As he stands up from between my legs, he puts a paper towel over the instruments on the tray beside him. I wonder what he's hiding, what I'm not supposed to see. Has he done something to me that isn't part of the regular exam? Something my mom would know was wrong if she saw under that paper towel. Would she even care at this point?

The three of us are in the room now: the doctor and my mom, both fully clothed, stand eye to eye. I sit on the exam table naked from the waist down with nothing but an oversized paper towel to cover me.

"Karen indicated that her plan is to terminate this pregnancy. I will give you the necessary paperwork to have that procedure done at a clinic."

"Is there any reason why she couldn't have the pregnancy terminated here?" my mom asks.

"I do perform the procedure, but only with a local anesthetic. My recommendation is that she is treated at a clinic that will perform this procedure under general anesthesia."

I don't have any idea what he is talking about. I know it has something to do with hospitals. It seems to me that local is best so the pain is stopped at the source, instead of general, where I may feel slightly better all over, like with aspirin.

"But aren't some of those clinics unsafe? How do I know she will be treated by a *real* doctor?"

"Plenty of girls like Karen are treated at clinics," he says.

It's clear to my mom and me what he means by "girls like Karen." My mom sternly says "Thank you" indicating that she no longer needs to speak to him. They both leave the room and I am left alone to wipe up lubricating jelly still smeared between my legs and get dressed.

Back in the car, all doubts have been erased. Yes, I'm pregnant. Yes, I'm one of *those girls*. Yes, it's been determined that I will have an abortion. Staring straight ahead, I don't want to catch my mom's disappointed glances. I can't look out the side window because if one stranger smiles at me right now, I'll start crying and never stop. All the music coming through the radio sounds hollow, from a different time. It's not the soundtrack from my present, because I'm so changed, but it's too current to be the soundtrack from my past.

When we get back home I wonder out loud where my dad and brother have been all day, but my mom does not volunteer information. Back on the phone in front of the big phone book, my mom is answering questions.

"Yes, she has a positive pregnancy test from a doctor." Mom listens on the phone.

"Approximately eight weeks pregnant." Her answers are all business.

"She would like the first available appointment." After saying this, there is a long pause as she listens, her face revealing her irritation, her exasperation.

"If she already has a pregnancy test and she's already made the decision, why does she need to come in for counseling beforehand?" With a pen she draws deep lines on the phone book page while listening to the person on the other end of the line. The opposite of a "lifeline."

"Fine, we will be there tomorrow at 10 a.m." She looks like she lost a week's worth of sleep during that call.

"First you have to go in and have a counseling session with them, and then wait 48 hours."

Frustrated, defeated and helpless, all I can muster up is a simple "Thanks Mom."

She doesn't say anything back. But really, what she's supposed to say? *"You're welcome, no problem, let's do it again sometime."* I get up from the bed to walk out of the room, half expecting her to tell me I'm not allowed to leave. Every move made now is tentative. I never know what my parents are thinking; never know what the next rule will be. Sometimes they want to keep me close and sometimes they don't want to see my face at all.

The next morning my dad and my brother are out of the house before I'm out of my room. My mom is at the living room desk making work phone calls. I know she's mad that I'm causing her to miss so much time from work. Waiting 'til she hangs up the phone, I ask,

"Do you need anything?" but all I get is her blank stare.

"I'll be in my room then."

There's nowhere in my house that I feel at home.

The clinic isn't like the doctor's office, it's much more crowded and the girls are younger, although I'm still the youngest one. My mom is obviously humiliated to be here. I think the only reason she doesn't wait in the car is because she wants to ensure that I go through with this. When my name is called my mom gets up with me, but a lady who's much too young to be a nurse tells my mom that they need to talk to me alone. I can feel the anger vibrating off my mom's body. For a moment her posture becomes rigid, but then she sits back down, assuming her perfectly poised posture on the chair.

I hand over my paperwork indicating that I am, in fact, pregnant. There are forms that need to be filled out and signed by me. Even though I'm not an adult and can't really enter into a legal agreement, the people here want to make sure that this is my choice and I am not being forced into it. I'm not 100% certain that's the case, but I can't see any other way, I don't have any other CHOICE, so I sign the papers. This is what I need to do to NOT be pregnant.

Someone who looks more like a nurse explains there are two ways they do this at the clinic. One is when you're completely asleep, called general anesthesia. The other is when you're only numb from the waist down, called local anesthesia. I understand now why the first doctor sent me away, he wanted me to be asleep for the procedure. The nurse from the clinic explains that being asleep costs more money, but there is paperwork to fill out for financial assistance. She says I only have a few weeks before they will no longer be able to do it at their facility because I'm already eight weeks along.

"Do you have any questions?" the nurse asks.

I wish I could ask her how to talk to my mom, or how to stop the sadness. I want to ask her how to get Jack to hold some of this burden upon his shoulders. She can't care, with a hundred more girls to see today, I'm one out of many, taking up more than my share of time. All I can manage to ask her is, "Will I be able to have children later, when I'm ready, when I'm older?"

It's then that tears finally come. I love children. I made this child in love, I'm killing it out of fear.

When I come out to the waiting area my mom simply asks, "Are we done here?"

"Yeah."

"Fine," she says, her lips pursed, lines so deep forming between her eyebrows I don't know if she will ever become un-creased.

It's not 'til we are back in the car and driving home that she asks, "Why were you crying?"

"Because I'm sad Mom, it's not like I don't have feelings."

"You should've thought of that before you started having sex."

The next two nights my mind spins me awake, imagining all my "options". Could I give the baby up for adoption? What if the people who adopted were abusive? I could steal my baby back. Maybe I could live with Jack and his mom, and we can all be a family together? I haven't even heard from Jack since the night they listened to our phone call. I could run away, live on the streets. That would be fine for me, but not for my baby. Isn't there some program for pregnant teenage fourteen-year-olds?

The solution always returns to: do whatever you have to do to not be pregnant anymore. It is probable that any other option will end tragically.

Not once in my life did my parents ever have a "facts of life" talk with me, other than my mom telling me "If you ever find some blood on your panties, don't be scared, just come and tell me". The facts of life. Yeah right.

Here are the facts of my life:

The abortion is scheduled.

I will be shown mercy with the luxury of a general anesthesia.

My dad hasn't spoken to me since they first confronted me about being pregnant.

Jack hasn't made any attempt to contact me.

Gina will be moving away to a boarding school at the end of the month. She does not seem sad about leaving me. I can assume she sees me as a killer and will never love me like a friend again.

At the clinic I see everyone matched up in pairs. One person who is sad, scared; the other one a driver, the chaperone. There is a thirty-ish- year old couple, both nervously twisting their wedding bands while they wait, as if they are so much more aware of the rings around their fingers, or maybe they want everyone else to be. Next, a frightened looking twenty-year-old girl, and her relieved-looking companion who looks to be about 30. Across from me are two girls, probably eighteen or nineteen-years old, chatting and looking at magazines like they are waiting on a manicure appointment. I am the youngest girl here and the only one who seems to have her parent as her co-pilot. I am also the only one who has the problem of tears sneaking past the weak dam of my eyelids.

When my name is called, my mom doesn't even try to come in with me. She stares straight ahead as I follow the nurse to a cubicle where I'm told to write out in my own handwriting that I consent to having an abortion. From there it is time to abandon my clothes. I am given a paper gown, hair bonnet and paper shoes to wear. I'm led to another room to sit and wait.

The next waiting room is cold; I try my best to pull the paper gown tight around me, but it provides no comfort or shield. The perimeter of the room is lined with seats divided by wooden arm rests. There are ten other girls in this room, lined up like paper cutouts, waiting for the same reason. Girls just like me, telling ourselves this will all be over soon. I want to trade my grief with relief.

I feel guilty for wanting to feel relieved.

Every time a name is called she walks slowly out of the room and doesn't come back. Eventually her seat is taken by another paper doll. When they call my name, I know this is it; my last chance to turn around and run. Once through those doors, I'm past the point of no return.

I enter the coldest room, silver and gray; it puts a medicinal taste in my mouth like the smell of Band-Aids. There are four stainless steel tables in a row with poles reaching up from both sides at the end. A girl is lying on one of the tables, slightly curled in the fetal position, moaning, a paper sheet covering her from the waist down. The next table has a girl lying on her back, giant rubber bands looped around her knees have them spread wide and high, hanging from the outside of the bars at the edge of that table. She is also covered from the waist down with a paper sheet, but she is sleeping, not making a sound. I'm led to the long, gun-metal gray table and told to get up onto it. Trying my best to keep myself covered with my thin paper robe, the nurse has no patience for my time-consuming modesty. The moment my ass hits the cold table, I'm swarmed by strangers. I don't know where they came from.

"Lie down and scoot to the edge please," a woman says, as she takes her position between my legs.

"Come down a little more." I shimmy to the end of the table.

"Scoot down some more." I move so my butt feels like it's hanging off the table.

"OK. Good," she says finally as she slips those big rubber bands over my feet and up to my knees.

There's another lady at my side who has strapped my wrist to the table and stuck my elbow pit with a needle connected to a tube, taping that to my arm. A third lady to my right has opened up my paper gown and is sticking little electrodes on my chest.

Overwhelmed and shaking, it feels like I've been kidnapped. The table is ice cold and sends pain through my ribs. Sadness and darkness come over my heart like a hard shell to protect me from what I am about to do.

The women begin to chat with each other about their plans for after work. I'm lying cold, watching as the moaning girl is rolled from the room and the sleeping girl begins to wake and groan. A man's voice off to the side says he's ready and the conversation between the nurses stops. They direct their attention back down to me.

"Okay," says the lady to my left with the needle, "I want you to count down from 20 and this will all be over soon."

"20, 19, 18." I feel the woman grab one of my legs and pull up, strapping the giant rubber band that is wrapped around my knee and hooking it to the top of the pole. Like a side of beef hung up and about to be sawn in half.

"17, 16, 15." The lady to my right has grabbed the rubber band attached to my other knee and pulled my leg wide and up high. I am a wishbone, about to be broken. I feel the medicine come in through the needle; burning fire climbing up inside my arm. A hot burn, then cold; like death running through my veins.

"14, 13, 12." I am spread open like a Thanksgiving turkey; a man in a white coat suddenly appears and is now standing between my legs. One of the nurses is talking to him, saying medical things. It sounds like a different language.

"11, 10, 9…."

My own whimpering wakes me. Balled in the fetal position, they roll me into another place, like I am on a conveyor belt. This room is warmer. Some girls are sitting, others lying. Every five minutes another one comes out of a dressing room wearing their own clothes, like a person you'd see on the street. No longer a girl "just like me" —a hollow person with a shell of blue paper. She is granted her identity back.

"You are going to have to stop crying if you want to get dressed and go home," a nurse says to me offhand.

So this is it? If I can act like everything is fine, and sit up, I get to walk out of here? It's my sadness they are waiting to subside, not these cramps, not the bleeding.

"Can I get up and get dressed now?" I ask.

I must dry my tears and get through this. Maybe when I pass through that door, I will be like any other fourteen-year-old; maybe the sadness will go away. I'm no longer sentenced to drag another person through this fucked up life, but the weight of the world has not been cut from my body.

In the back seat of my mom's Oldsmobile, I cry. The loss of a future I've wanted and had to deny is a cloud of smoke that I keep brushing away; it returns, swarming dense and black, filling my head. I calm myself for a moment, but then cramps pull me back to reality, back to what I have done, what I have lost.

"You need to stop crying before we get home, your dad and brother will be there." My mom is so cold, she doesn't care that I am sad. "What am I supposed to tell your principal at school? How am I supposed to explain your absence?"

"Why don't you tell them that I'm a slut and that I missed school to have an abortion?" I say bitterly.

"That's perfect. That's exactly what I'll do," she says.

I'm not sure if she's being mean or serious. I am sure she hates me and can never forgive me. She never gave me a choice. I guess she hates that she had to make me do this.

18 • SLEDGEHAMMER

I'm sitting at my desk trying to focus on homework, but instead listing all the names my baby could have had. The Dead Kennedys' "Fresh Fruit for Rotting Vegetables" album is playing on my stereo. I love the way this music rumbles and grows, sounding evil and menacing. The meaning behind the political lyrics eludes me, but whenever I ask my mom about them, she gets angry and wants to know why I'm asking about such things.

Lost in my own world of music and writing, a loud crash jolts my focus. At first the noise seems to belong to the music, but my room is shaking as if an earthquake is splitting walls in half and crashing in. It's not the walls, but the door. Pieces of the door are flying toward me. There's a sledgehammer in my dad's hand; my mom is standing right behind him.

"What are you doing? What's going on?" I'm compelled to walk towards the door but I know that's the wrong idea.

"If you won't unlock this door I'll take the lock off!" He's screaming, spit flying from his red face.

"Dad, I didn't even hear you knock! I have the stereo on. Calm down!"

"No one can be calm with this music playing!" he screams as he raises the sledgehammer again. He smashes the stereo. I can't believe my eyes. It's like he is killing off my best friend, my only friend in this house.

It was only a year ago my dad finished building this stereo into the wall. Each component set perfectly inside the wall on glass shelves. No wires visible, so everything looks seamless, modern, like the Jetsons. He's just smashed it all to bits. What the hell is wrong with him? Why can't he simply turn the volume down like a normal parent? It's raining glass and metal; a fog of drywall dust fills the entrance of my room. The floor is eventually covered with bits of everything he's smashed—glittery glass, toothpick-sized wooden shards, wires and electrical parts from the stereo's insides — my dead robot buddy.

My parents completely invade my room and sit down on my bed. Isn't removing my door enough? Can't they leave now that he's done? I guess we've only just begun.

"What are you doing?" my mom asks.

"Homework." I'm hoping my answer is enough to make them leave. What did they think they would catch me doing in my room?

"We've been reading some of your writing." My mom says in her matter-of-fact tone. The tone she uses to remind me she is always in control of the field, no matter what game is being played. I wonder when they were snooping around in my room and what they got their hands on. What do they know exactly?

"We want to see your tattoo."

My heart is forty pounds of their disappointment falling into my stomach. They know about my tattoo.

I pull off my sock and show them the world's smallest tattoo, the world's most harmless tattoo, the easiest tattoo in the world to hide. So easy, in fact, that I've had it for weeks without them knowing. They only found out by snooping around. A simple circle, a Germs symbol. It sat there looking innocent enough to me.

o

"Is that the same place that Jack tattooed Tammy's foot?" my mom asks.

"Huh? What are you talking about?"

"Tammy's mother called to warn us about Jack. Apparently, he held Tammy down and tattooed his initials on her foot."

"That's impossible! This tattoo is a hundred little dots of ink. It took me an hour to do this. There is no way Jack gave Tammy a tattoo. She must have done it to herself. I gave Tammy my India ink a few days ago."

"So you taught Tammy how to tattoo herself?" No matter what I say, my mom will always make *me* out to be the villain. Is Tammy a villain? Is she fucking Jack?

"We also read that you smoke cigarettes, and that you want to have a girlfriend. Is this true?" My mom looks more sad than mad now.

"I don't know what you want me to say, Mom."

"What have we done to cause this? Say this isn't true!" My dad is being dramatic again, getting himself all wound up.

"Come on Dad, you have a tattoo, I have a tattoo. You smoke, Mom smokes, everyone around me smokes. I smoke. I'm sorry I'm growing up to be just like you." I wonder if this will work, see if they can process this logically and move on. Maybe this is how Jack got his mom to accept him? I think for him it has more to do with the fact that he's bigger than her so she feels threatened.

"Is that it? I smoke, so you smoke? I'm not going to concede to that! I refuse to accept that!" My dad jumps up from the bed and storms out of the room. I'm relieved to see him go. Perhaps the drama is 50% over.

Nope.

My dad comes back in my room holding his carton of cigarettes. Pulling out a pack and opening it, he starts cracking, smashing, crumbling cigarettes onto my carpet, making another mess on my bedroom floor. He grabs the next pack and does the same thing. I can't stand these theatrics. I'd really like a cigarette. I've never smoked in front of my parents before, but right now seems like the perfect time to start.

There's an unbroken cigarette on the floor mixed in the pile of broken ones. All the loose tobacco falling onto my carpet, I'm staring at that one cigarette, daring myself to grab it. My dad is getting himself so worked up, he is almost crying.

"I would give anything to keep you in good health, to spare you from the treachery of smoking, to save you from this horrible habit." My dad is acting—who is that notoriously horrible actor? Richard Burton? William Shatner? My dad is the William Shatner of parenting. No matter how many cigarettes he smashes, or what he says or promises, he's still going to leave my room and light up. And I'm still going to take that one good cigarette from the pile and smoke it when I can. He's wasting all these cigarettes I can't afford.

So they know about the tattoo, and they know about the smoking, and they know about Dominique. What else did I write down? Let's get this conversation to move along to the end. Dish out the punishment and leave me alone.

My mom is pretty much done with all the drama and lays out her solution. I will be dropped off and picked up from school. I am not allowed out on the weekends. They will take the phone out of my room. In spite of the fact that my stereo was murdered, they remove every album they deem "Punk Rock". They don't care that most don't belong to me and I need to return them. Somehow *I* have the anger problem because of my music, tattoos and "attitude". No one discusses my dad taking a sledgehammer to the door or the stereo he custom-built into my wall. Hypocrites.

A prisoner in my own room, I feel crazy because I have no say in what's going to happen to me. No control. Tammy tattoos her foot, I suffer the consequences. I'm honest with my parents about smoking, but they can't accept it. Nothing in this house is going to change. I'm certain they don't like me, and not even really sure if they love me. It's time for me to get out. I can do better on my own.

I've managed to save $30 and I stuff it into my backpack along with a change of clothes, my toothbrush, and Sherman, the stuffed elephant I've slept with since I was a kid.

If I still had a stereo in my room "Too Young to Die" would be playing. It's the soundtrack for what I'm about to do and the song playing in my head as I walk past the ruins of my bedroom door.

♫ I've learned from my mistakes,
This time I will escape,
I'm too young to die.♫

At three o'clock in the morning the house is quiet. My backpack is my parachute as I slowly, finally, close the door to their house behind me. Barefoot with my skates in my hand, I run far enough away to hide and tie them on my feet. It figures that it's raining. All sad and dramatic parts in movies start out this way. I'm not sad though. I feel excited, hopeful, like my real life is just about to start.

Roller-skating in the rain is not as bad as I anticipated. Once I commit to it, it's fun. Visually, skating in the rain is like riding in a car while it's snowing. Skating towards the rain, it looks like it's coming at me at an angle, like I'm skating into a tunnel. I've surrendered to the fact that I'm going to be wet, and I'm not cold. As my clothes become wet and heavy with rain, my body is warming from skating, so I'm basically the same temperature as when I started. Skating on the slick pavement makes a cartoon sound effect; *whoosh whoosh*. I am fast and invincible.

I skate the two miles to Van and Tim's house. Jack and I have snuck into the trailer parked in their driveway a few times before to have sex. Luckily it's unlocked and I curl up under the blankets of the little bed like Goldilocks, like a burglar. Every little noise seems amplified. I wonder if my parents woke up when I closed their door behind me. If I'm discovered in this trailer, will I be kicked out or will my parents be called? In four more hours, I can call Jack; 'til then I'll stay still. He'll know what to do. I wonder what he'll say when I tell him I finally ran away?

19 ● RUNAWAY

Just after sunrise, I slip out of the little trailer in the driveway and knock on the small garage window. Tim opens the door and doesn't seem particularly happy to see me. The yellow and orange hues of sunrise reveal pillowcase lines still embedded on his face.

Van and Tim live in their parents' garage. At some point the brothers had gotten in enough trouble that their folks decided to sequester them away from the rest of the family and leave them to themselves. They are allowed in the house to get what they need from the kitchen and to use the bathroom. It seems like the perfect situation to me, a roof over your head and no one telling you what to do. I wonder how I can get my parents to do the same.

Van gets out of bed and the two sit down to take a hit from the ever-present bong on the table.

"What are you doing here?" Tim asks.

"Jack isn't here," Van adds.

"I ran away from home last night and I had nowhere to go. I snuck into your trailer."

I'm hoping they'll tell me I can stay there again tonight, but that offer never comes. The only thing they offer is a bong hit, which I decline.

"You can't stay in there. My dad will call the cops if he finds you," Tim says.

"I'm sorry, I won't do it again. Can I stay in here with you guys until I can call Jack?"

Lucky for me, they acquiesce.

To create makeshift room dividers, signs are hanging haphazardly in their garage, signs no longer needed from their dad's failed political campaign. The red, white and blue cardboard signs say

"Blunt for Governor". I chuckle at the irony as I read them through clouds of pot smoke. Their garage always smells like weed and I wonder if that is part of why their dad didn't achieve his political goals.

They have the same Farrah Fawcett poster on their wall that I had, the one that caused a debate between my mom and a family friend about whether or not it was an indication that I was gay. It didn't matter that right next to it on my wall was an Andy Gibb poster. Everybody has one of those Farrah Fawcett posters. It just feels good to have her smile at you like that.

I barely have time to finish my sandwich when Van says in a panic, "Get under my covers!" He grabs my arm and leads me to hide under all the clothes piled on his bed. Their mom opens the door and says in a tired, monotone voice, "You boys need to get off your asses and look for jobs today or sign up to get your G.E.D.s." It's obvious to me, by the sound of her voice, that this is an empty threat. All feeling is missing from the words, like she is reading an obligatory script and she knows once she closes the door they won't have to consider her wishes again until she comes home. She never comments about the bong on the coffee table. I find it odd that they have to hide me, but not their pot.

Once both parents leave, Van goes into the house to call Jack. He returns with a sandwich for me. I normally don't eat this early, but the food is welcome as I don't know where my next meal is coming from, and I tell them as much.

"How much money do you have?" Van asks.

"Thirty dollars" I say proudly.

"That's not going to get you far," Tim says, deflating my lofty bubble.

"Jack says he'll be here soon as he can." Van's words end Tim's criticism of me, and remind me that Jack is my solution; he will know what to do.

Van and Tim go off to talk privately in a section of the garage barricaded by plywood and blankets and more "Blunt for Governor" signs. I can't hear anything they say. Eating my charity breakfast, I take a long look at my surroundings.

Heaps of magazines form a geological site. I slowly unearth a bit at a time, unveiling the last year of their lives. The surface, being the most recent, is nothing more than beer caps, burned matches, bits of weed that fell off the rolling tray and High Times magazine. The layer hidden underneath (maybe six months prior) shows more hope for their lives and more general interest in life: concert ticket stubs, a paycheck stub, and rock 'n roll magazines featuring bands like RUSH and Black Sabbath; even newspaper clippings about their dad's run for office.

Sadness struck me when I found the faded, soiled photographic proof these boys were once part of a family of five. Their mom looked so hopeful, holding her newborn; dad looked so proud with his arms around his two sons.

I can't imagine what allows them to leave stuff on a coffee table for so long. An entire year's history is at my fingertips. Nothing put back where it belongs, nothing ever completely finished. It seems they are unable to make the simple decision of whether or not they are done with reading a magazine, or whether a shirt should be hung up or put in the hamper. Things are left in a state of chaotic limbo, everything left so accessible that eventually nothing is. If you are no longer expected to determine if something is clean or dirty, how can you possibly decide something as profound as "I am dropping out of school"?

At what point do parents decide they are done with their kids? Is it for the kid's protection or the parents'? Once they move their child to the garage like the family pet, is it possible for the kid to really dream of becoming a doctor or lawyer? Like a goldfish kept in a small bowl, at some point does your environment limit your potential? Is living in a garage better or worse than being on the streets? If you're out in society you are forced to fight to survive; your "will to live" is kept intact. Kept cozy in a garage, I imagine your survival instinct becomes dulled and you become content being nothing but stoned on the couch all day. A roof over your head is not a home. Van and Tim weren't free or lucky. And just because they were indoors didn't mean they were safe.

Back from their private conversation, Tim hands me a plastic baggy half-full of green and red capsules.

"What's this?" I ask.

"Christmas trees," Van says.

"Speed," Tim clarifies.

"I don't take speed," I tell them. "I'm hyper already."

"They're for you to sell, for money," Van is happy to be helpful.

"But you can't tell Jack." Tim is serious about this.

"Why not?" I don't understand.

"He'd eat them," Tim explains.

"Yeah, he'd probably take them all at once," Van laughs.

"You can sell them for two or three dollars apiece. There are sixty in this bag. Come back with sixty dollars cash for me and I'll give you more to sell," Tim explains the deal.

I'm not certain I can hide things from Jack, but I cram the pills deep in the bottom of my backpack under Sherman, hopeful that I can make some money.

Jack doesn't arrive with the urgency I expected. I imagined him rushing to me, wrapping me in his arms and telling me everything was going to be okay. I wanted him to hold me and tell me he'll take care of me. Instead he walks in, kisses me on the forehead, flops down on the couch and announces to Van and Tim, "Looks like your parents are gone, let's smoke a joint."

Van reluctantly rolls a joint, explaining that after they smoke, we have to leave so they can get busy looking for jobs. I can't imagine looking for a job stoned, or doing anything stoned.

I've only smoked pot once, two years ago, when my 6th grade best friend Stacey and I were twelve. Stacey's 19 year-old sister, Shelly and her boyfriend got us stoned while their parents went out. I liked the way the pot made my body feel, taking away my arthritic pain. I loved how it made ice cream taste so much more amazing and sweet but hated the way the marshmallows of the rocky road felt slimy in my mouth. I didn't like the way pot made me feel stupid and incapable of making swift decisions or expressing myself, which was necessary the moment Stacey and Shelly left the room and the 19-year-old boyfriend started coming on to me. Yeah, I had been flirting with him, like I do with everyone, but I was dumbstruck when he stroked my hair and kissed my lips. His gross hippy facial hair rubbed roughly against my cheeks. His disgusting and unwanted advances stopped before I could even imagine what to say to him.

Once Jack is high, he rescues me from my unhappy thoughts and says "Let's go."

"You can leave your backpack in my garage and pick it up later," Tim says.

Jack thinks they are being nice to me, but I know they don't want me to get busted wandering around with their speed in my backpack. They care more about those pills than me, and I don't blame them; they hardly know me. They're taking a big risk in investing so much in me.

As we leave the garage, Jack whispers, "Let's go fuck in the trailer, we have to hide from the truant officers somewhere."

"What's a truant officer? Are there actual police looking for kids that aren't in school? What's the point of being out of school all day if we can't go anywhere or do anything?" I ask, pissed.

"They don't have big fat joints at school," he says and grabs me, finally giving me the passionate kiss I've been waiting for all morning. "We can't do *that* when you're at school."

Sometimes Jack is so romantic; the look in his eyes is so sincere. It feels as if my whole world will implode if he left. At this moment, I know that the only thing that gives me breath is his belief in my existence. I don't even register on this planet to anyone else. Without Jack, I would simply evaporate. Moments like this are what I live for.

"What about Van and Tim?" I am the nervous sissy.

"If they catch us, we'll grab your backpack and head towards the beach. If they don't catch us, we have the trailer to ourselves and when were done, we'll get your backpack and head towards the beach. Either way, they can't be mad at us. Who can resist young lovers?"

I suppose he's right, and I want his undivided attention.

Making out with Jack is a nice distraction from my over-crowded brain. When we kiss I feel as if I am breathing him in, eating his essence. I imagine that enough of our spit will exchange and eventually we will become more of each other.

After making love, my body is relaxed, like I didn't know my muscles were clenched but now they've let go. My mind is still crowded, thoughts fill and burst like soap bubbles: "What if I get arrested by a truant officer? What if I get an infection from having sex so soon after the abortion? What if Van and Tim return and take the speed from me—the only way I have to make any money. It takes less than five minutes for my body to return to tight, alert, panicked. Fight or flight mode.

"I can't see the point in being on my own if my life isn't improved. I don't want to waste my days doing nothing, waiting for my life to begin. I have already been waiting for love and understanding and sanity for so long. Tomorrow morning I am going to go to school." School seems like a safe place, a place to hide from my parents and get food and shelter. At school I can relax for seven hours a day. (I can also sell speed to the rich kids in school, but I didn't say that out loud.)

"Your parents will grab you from there and take you home," he warns.

"They don't want me to drop out. I can't imagine them grabbing me from class." School seems like a simple solution to me.

Jack asks, "What am I supposed to do all day?"

"You should go to school too. Do it because they expect us NOT to." I try to inspire him. I want so badly to save us both. "I'm gonna do it because they *don't* expect me to succeed."

With a plan I find myself relaxed, almost content. All the bubbles in my head that pop release the words "I'll show them". I fall to sleep in my lover's arms knowing everything is as it should be. I'm not sure how long we nap before we wake to the sound of the trailer door opening and a man, Mr. Almost Governor I guess, is yelling.

"Get out of here! You have one minute to put your clothes on and get out or I'm calling the cops!"

Scrambling to get out of bed, I get tied up in the sheets, like I'm caught in a net. The more I rush to get out of bed and get dressed the longer it seems to take. Jack doesn't seem to rush at all, he's moving at the same easy pace he always does, cool; like Fonzie.

I tumble out of the trailer door and Mr. Blunt stands there with his arms crossed. I don't know what I expected a prospective Governor to look like, but this man just looks like a Dad, a pissed off Dad. I feel awful, like I have personally violated this man's home.

"I'm sorry. Please don't call the police. We didn't hurt anything," I say as I stumble past him.

"I am locking this place up tight so don't bother coming back!" he warns.

Jack saunters out behind me. "What's up Mr. Blunt? How you doing?"

"Oh it's *you*; I should've known you were behind this. This isn't your love shack, Jack. Why don't you stay away from me and my boys?" There's sadness and tenderness in Mr. Bunt's voice that is incongruent with his words. He seems to care about Jack and they have some kind of history. I'm not sure how long Jack has known this family, but when Mr. Blunt says, "That's quite a look you have going on there buddy," I figure he's known Jack since before he was a punk.

"Thanks, let me know when you want me to come by and do *your* hair." They both chuckle and Jack convinces him to let us in the garage so I can get my backpack. How does Jack get this man to laugh and help us after we've snuck into his trailer? I'm afraid to talk to most adults, but Jack can charm everyone, except *MY* parents.

We walk the three miles back to Jack's apartment. His mom's fridge is full of delicious food and we eat like it's our last meal before electrocution. It's only 1:00 in the afternoon and already I've got a bag of speed pills and "ditched" my first day of school ever. I've had to hide from the cops, run away from my friends' dad (even if he was then charmed by Jack), and made love to my boyfriend in a sun-filled trailer. It seems I've done a lot, but I haven't done anything. Anxiety returns again, a tornado spinning inside my chest and mind. I'm just sitting around, but I want something magnificent to happen. Anticlimactic.

This feeling reminds me of the first time I rode on an airplane when I was seven years old. I was so excited and got all dressed up in my new, pale blue, polyester pantsuit. When I got to the airport I had to wait, and then I got on the airplane and waited some more. Aside from the excitement of the airplane lifting off the ground, the actual ride was merely sitting for hours doing nothing. The landing part was exciting for maybe 60 seconds and then I was back on the runway waiting to taxi to the gate. I landed in an airport exactly like the one I left hours ago; nothing was different. Everyone told me it was gonna be some big adventure: "You're going on an airplane ride! How exciting!"

But it was really a bunch of waiting around and nothing

changed. I didn't feel any different, I wasn't treated any differently. I was still just a seven-year-old kid, carrying my dolls in a basket, pretending to be a grown-up in my polyester pantsuit.

I do the best I can to ignore the impending doom filling my head. When Jack's mom comes home, I stay in his room while he somehow convinces her to let me stay the night and not call my parents or the cops. I don't know if she likes me, I think she simply wants to keep Jack out of as much trouble as possible.

The next morning Jack walks with me a few blocks towards school.

"I'm not going all the way," he says. "Let's meet here after school."

I feel small, vulnerable and open to attack once I am alone on the street.

Tammy is waiting in the front of the school.

"Your mom called my house yesterday looking for you. Where'd you go?"

"Did you tattoo Jack's initials on your foot with my India ink?" I demand.

"Why would I do that?" Tammy asks, holding my gaze as she hands me a sandwich.

Tammy is stealing my sanity right under my nose. Like the cashier in the drugstore, I am thankful for her care and attention. Who do I believe? My parents who hate me and everyone I want to be friends with, or Tammy, my friend who thinks about my needs and brings me food? I bite into the sandwich, resigned not to ask about the tattoo again. The truth will be revealed; a tattoo isn't going to go away.

"Where did you go yesterday?"

"I ran away in the middle of the night, got kicked out of a trailer by a Governor, and spent the night at my boyfriend's house." When put that way, even I was impressed with how my adventure sounded.

Tammy's curiosity is obviously stoked, but then her expression quickly changes as she looks past me.

"There's your mom!" She says in a panic.

I follow Tammy's line of vision to the curb 20 feet away. My mom is getting out of her car and heading towards me.

"Oh shit! What do I do?" I feel frozen. Isn't this a normal thing, to stand in front of your school before the bell rings in the morning? Why do I feel like I've been caught doing something wrong? My eyes meet with my mom's. I can't tell if she's mad at me, or happy to see me alive. I can't read her expression that far away. Often I couldn't read her expression when we were sitting across the dinner table from each other.

"Run!" Tammy says, and that seems like the right thing to do.

I break the stare between me and my mom, spin and run down the sidewalk of P.C.H. I don't want to return to Jack's house. If I lead my parents there and they call the cops, Jack's mom will never let me back in. I'm running away from the school and the bell is gonna ring in a few minutes and then I won't be allowed in. I've crossed two streets and I can't recall if the lights were green. Heart pounding, breathing heavy, my eyes feel big and wide like they have been forced open; the opposite of being stoned.

After a few blocks, I realize to continue running is increasing my chances of being seen on the street. I duck behind some bushes in front of a medical building, crouched in five square feet of wilderness on the busiest highway in Redondo Beach. I look down to my hand and see that I've never let go of the PB&J Tammy gave me. Unclenching my fist, turning my palm towards the dirt, the brown wad with sticky grape spots won't release; it's stuck like Play-Doh. I flick my hand and the bulk of it flies into the bush, leaving a mess that I have nothing to clean it with. Pulling my sock up to my knee, I wipe my hand on it, and scrunch it back down towards my purple high-top. I'm going to have to remember to start wearing two pairs of socks at once from now on.

What's mom doing now? Is she running down the street looking for me? Is she waiting for me to come back to the school, so she can force me home like Jack predicted? Is she going into school to tell them not let me in? Is she at the police station reporting me as a runaway? Has she finally given up and driven off to start her day at work? Where's my dad? Maybe he's coming in from the other side and any minute they'll have me cornered. I can't sit here and hide all day. What do I want to do? How seldom that particular phrase goes through my head. In the past it's always been "What am I supposed to do" or "What do they want me to do." So here I am crouching in some bushes asking myself "What do I want to do?"

Sticking my head up over the bush I look around. I should feel comfort that the whole world is unaware of my existence, but I don't. Cautiously walking back to school, I try to calculate how much time has passed. In the count of heartbeats, I have spent an hour. Back at school it seems it's only been minutes; my group of friends are just now walking in. I fall in step with them, trying to catch my breath.

"Your mom told me she'll leave you alone at school, she's glad you're attending." Tammy tells me this as we walk past the school office and through our classroom door. The bell rings, I'm safe for the next seven hours.

We are settled into our desks no more than five minutes when Tammy passes me a note.

"How did you meet the Governor?"

"Let's talk at break," I whisper.

Another note— "Is Jack meeting you at lunch?"

"Let's talk at break!" I say a bit louder.

I refuse to put anything in writing, in case the teacher sees us. I don't want to talk with Tammy because I am still confused about the tattoo my boyfriend may have put on her foot. It takes several unanswered notes before she finally stops. Is she trying to get me in trouble?

At first break we walk to the far end of the playground.

I have something to discuss with her besides Jack.

"Have you ever heard of pills called Christmas Trees?"

"No, did you get them from the Governor?" Tammy asks.

"They're speed. If you know anyone that might buy them, I need to give this guy money for them."

"What do they do?" Tammy is very intrigued.

"They're like diet pills, they make you hyper and not hungry and awake I guess…. I've never taken one."

"Let me have one," Tammy says, bracelets jingling as she holds out her tiny manicured hand.

"O.K. but you have to help me *sell* them, I owe this guy money," I explain.

Tammy takes the pill and swallows it without anything to drink.

Back in class, I observe Tammy to see how the pill affects her. After an hour, her eyes look wild and her hands are fidgeting, but she says she feels great and asks for another one. "Shut up!" I say sternly in a half-whisper. "Let's talk at lunch." The last thing I need is to be caught selling drugs here. I want things to be normal at school, I should've never told Tammy about the pills; at least not right away.

By the time I make it through the lunch line and sit down at the table, people are coming up and asking me about the pills. I don't know how she does it, but Tammy can sell anything, or convince people that a bad idea is good. Are these pills really a bad idea? Anyone can buy diet pills at the grocery store. Kids are buying them from me like they know what they are. I can't imagine every one of them would pop a pill in their mouth that they've never seen before like Tammy. These kids are all older than me and they are not my responsibility. By the end of lunch I have enough money to repay Van and Tim. I'm disappointed that Jack didn't show up at lunch to see me; he's probably afraid of my parents showing up. If he was standing around at the fence I wouldn't have been able to sell the speed anyway. At the end of lunch I take the money I made and put it inside my jeans pocket and stuff the rest of the pills deep into my backpack. I wish my school had lockers so I could leave the money and pills at school, away from Jack.

I meet Jack at our designated spot.

"How was your day at the office, dear?" He smiles and kisses me on my lips.

"Lovely, my mom showed up at the beginning, but I ran away."

"So where have you been all day long?" Jack asks.

"At school. I ran away and then came back. My mom told Tammy that she would leave me alone while I'm at school."

"No way. I can't believe she didn't grab you."

"Well, at first she couldn't catch me, and then I guess she didn't want to." I feel a bit sad when I say this, and for a moment I consider how my mom might've felt as I ran away from her. I push that thought away with the memory of my dad smashing my door in with a sledgehammer while my mom stood behind him.

Jack takes me to see his friend Tricia, a twenty-year-old punk who lives in a cool bungalow near my school. She has dirty hair and messy makeup and postures herself more like a boy than a girl. She seems happy to see Jack, but doesn't even acknowledge me. Her house is dirty, clothes everywhere, dishes piled in the kitchen. Her roommate rents from her, so she's the boss.

"You can crash on my couch tonight if you wash my dishes and put all these clothes in a garbage bag." Tricia says with a bit of a British accent.

"She's a local South Bay girl," Jack says when she leaves. "She just got back from a trip to England"

"How cool." I gush. I've never been anywhere.

When she's gone we do her chores and Jack drinks one of the two beers in the fridge.

"I can't drink them all," he says "She's an alcoholic and would go fucking crazy."

Tricia's roommate Joe comes home. He is a bookish, nerdy, dude who seems annoyed when Jack informs him we are staying the night.

"Aw, don't look so sad, Joe," Jack says. "I'll stack K.P. on top of me so we don't take up much space."

Joe leers at me, imagining what that might look like.

"We were just leaving," Jack says, which is news to me. Why can't we stop for a minute? I am already tired of running.

"We'll be back later with a joint." Jack says. He does seem to know what everyone wants.

"That sounds cool." Joe is suddenly excited.

Out the door and out of earshot I ask Jack how old Joe is.

"I think he's 28."

Joe's enthusiasm that my boyfriend almost half his age is going to bring some weed seems odd to me. Guess Joe's a late bloomer.

20 • GROWING WILD

Being the first one up in the house has never felt as lonely as it does today. I tiptoe into the bathroom to take a shower. The water comes out brown at first and the old pipes rattle the house. I'm afraid of disturbing Tricia or Joe, but I have to get ready for school. The tile inside the shower is dirty and the grout is green with mold. If my skin touches the walls, I will be dirtier than when I got in.

I didn't ask permission to use Tricia's shower, let alone her toiletries. Thinking of my parents always saying "Don't over-stay your welcome", I get out of the shower as quickly as possible and put on the only other change of clothes in my backpack: a skirt, T-shirt and sweatshirt. At school we don't wear uniforms, but there is a strictly enforced dress code that dictates the girls wear skirts. I wear my purple high tops with my skirts every day.

I come out of the bathroom to find Tricia sitting on the edge of the couch, in the space where I was laying next to Jack, who is still asleep.

"Sorry Tricia, did I wake you?" my voice meek.

"Yup. Hand me that can of beer under the clothes by your feet," she demands.

"It's warm," I tell her. "Want me to put it in the fridge and bring you a cold one?"

"No, I left it out on purpose; I like warm beer in the morning. That's how we drink it in England. You know, a drop of baby oil rubbed over your hair will make it less frizzy." She puts the beer to her mouth and tilts her head back, taking a big chug.

"Thanks! Do you have any baby oil?"

"Nope." She tosses the empty beer can triumphantly across the room towards the kitchen. It passes inches from my head, but I'm sure if she meant to hit me, she would have. "Now run along or you'll be late for school." She flops down on her back, so now she is lying next to Jack. The only way I can kiss him goodbye is if I stretch my body across her; she has become the great barrier.

Grabbing my backpack, I head for the door. *"Don't look back, don't look back,"* I repeat in my mind as I walk away. I can't keep letting her fuck with me. I try to catch a glimpse of them reflected in the glass on the kitchen door, but instead her eyes meet mine in our reflections. Maybe I'm imagining it. It doesn't matter anyway.

Tricia's house is close to my school. If I could somehow get her and Joe to like me, perhaps we could stay there long enough for me to finish up the school year.

The usual crew is hanging out. Tammy, in her six inch stilettos, shorter than everyone else, but obviously the ring leader. When I walk up, conversation stops abruptly. They're all anticipating the current saga update. Seems like everyone knows I'm not living at home now. I beg them to quit talking about it, quit talking about me. Tammy wants more pills, so do other kids. I'm happy to have some money, but selling pills only complicates my precarious situation at school.

For P.E. we play volleyball, and I love the "normal" distraction. Tammy can run in high heels like a cartoon character, but during PE we have to wear tennis shoes and I am fascinated watching Tammy walk around on her tiptoes.

"Make your feet flat!" I laugh and tease her "Stand with your feet flat!"

"I can't, I swear I can't. This is as flat as they go." She's laughing at herself too.

"What are you talking about? You're too much of a girl? What the hell?" We're laughing so hard now that my stomach hurts as she tiptoes around the volleyball court. Whenever she hits the ball, it goes flying high and far into the air in some unexpected direction. We laugh even harder.

It's true, she simply can't walk with her feet flat on the ground in flat shoes. Because of her constant high-heel wearing, her calves have shortened, leaving her deformed. She thinks it's funny. It feels good to laugh. No one can make me laugh as hard as Tammy.

At lunchtime, I'm thankful for the food that Tammy brought me again. More kids I barely know come up asking for pills. I wonder if eventually one of them will be a spy, a "narc". Maybe the money I'm making isn't worth the risk. I look over at the girl who's always sitting next to that teacher, Mr. H, wearing his super tight blue PE shorts with white trim. Those two sit inappropriately close. Close enough for me to notice that she's always staring into his eyes and giggling. He's short, youngish and awkward and she's far too developed for his thoughts to be innocent. His ego swells in her attention so I know his thoughts aren't pure. If one of the kids told *her* I was selling pills, she would tell him; if only to seem more grown up in his eyes, or to be rewarded…somehow.

I have a lot to lose.

I have the most to lose.

When the final bell rings, Jack isn't at the front of the school. Walking back to Tricia's house, a sick feeling grows in my stomach. I'm not sure if I'm allowed over there, or welcome to knock on the door. Maybe it's nerves; am I jealous, or paranoid? Maybe my parents are following me, they know what time school gets out. Maybe I feel weird because I don't know what Jack's been up to all day. Am I just looking for things to worry about?

Jack answers my knock on Tricia's door. Assessing the room, I come to the conclusion that Jack and Joe have been on the couch, watching T.V. and drinking beer all day. The layer of pot smoke in the room keeps everything in soft focus. Joe's narrow eyes look like two tiny slits you couldn't even fit a dime in. He has a goofy look on his face like it's the first time he's ever been stoned and he's looking at me like he's never seen a girl before.

Jack grabs three beers from the refrigerator and tells me to sit down on the couch. Joe acts nervous when I sit down next to him. The slits of his eyes, when I look up close, are black dots surrounded by red.

"You went to school today?" Joe asked me.

"Yeah."

"So you're a good girl then?" He's relieved, like my soul is at stake.

"She's a bad girl who likes to be tied up and spanked," Jack volunteers, embarrassing Joe and me.

"Jack says you ran away from home, why?"

"Because my parents don't like me." Thinking I should be more positive I add, "I'm going to do much better on my own."

I walk over to the turntable and put the needle down on the Iggy and the Stooges Raw Power album. I read the song titles:

Search and Destroy
Gimme Danger
Your Pretty Face is Going to Hell
Penetration

The song titles read like the story of my life….

103

Raw Power
I Need Somebody
Shake Appeal
Death Trip...
Kinda funny how it ends.

"Do you have homework to do?" Joe is starting to sound like a dad.

"No, I get all my work done in school. It's easy." I don't need Joe to think of me as his daughter. That's a surefire way of him wanting me out of his house. He certainly won't want me drinking his beer or screwing my boyfriend on his couch.

I try to take a big dramatic drink like I saw Tricia do this morning, but the gulp seems to turn to solid in my throat and I kind of choke and hiccup all at once, causing beer to forcefully spray from my closed lips onto Joe's button up shirt.

Wanting to distract from my clumsiness and show that I have something to offer besides trouble for Joe, I try out a sexy move I've seen women do to men in movies a bunch of times before.

"Oh no, I'm so sorry, let me help you with that." I lean over and try to unbutton Joe's shirt.

Jack starts laughing and leans over to grab the bong.

"Come on, what are you, like, 16?" Joe asks.

"Back off K.P., you're coming on too strong. Don't you know you have to seduce him?" Jack hands the bong to Joe and says, "Why don't you take another hit?"

"Seduce me? No way, man, you're illegal!" Now Joe seems nervous and a lot less stoned. I'm not going to bother to tell him I'm only 14.

"Smoking pot is illegal, so is drinking with a minor, but you've been doing that all day."

"Yeah, well, I doubt I would go to prison for that."

"Quit making him feel like he's doing something wrong," Jack instructs.

I don't find Joe attractive. He's 28 and not exactly "cool". I need them both to pay attention to me, because they seem so content without me. Jack suggested I seduce Joe, and I agree it'll be harder for him to kick me out if he boinks me. I want to lie down between them and be worshipped. I'm lonely and empty and I want something to fill the void. Love me, please me, distract me, corrupt me.

"Sorry about your shirt Joe. I'm not trying to get you in trouble."

"There you go kids. Now kiss and make up," Jack says, pushing me into Joe.

I wrap my arms around Joe's shoulders and give him a hug, kissing him softly a few times on his cheek. He doesn't hug or kiss me back, but he doesn't push me away.

"I think she likes you, Joe," Jack says. "Don't you want to kiss her?"

"But she's *your* girlfriend," Joe says. "You're gonna let me kiss her?"

"*She's* gonna let you kiss her. I'm not worried about it. I hear Orientals have small dicks," Jack says with confidence, gripping his cock through his jeans.

"Yeah, but you're a boy, I'm a man," Joe says. I can almost see the blood return to his brain as he looks at me. "And *she's* just a kid."

"Aw Joe, I bet K.P.'s fucked more girls than you have. Why don't you come on in when you're ready?"

Jack leads me into Joe's room, I'd never been behind that door, but Jack walks in like he owns the place. I wonder if he and Joe were in there earlier today. Jack leaves the door open and pulls me down onto the bed. Joe can see us from his seat on the couch. Jack kisses me and it's definitely more exciting knowing that Joe's watching us from the other room. I moan loudly and I wonder if I'm doing it to put on a show for Joe or if I'm physically responding to the excitement. The sounds I'm making are matched by Jack as we writhe and press up against each other with our clothes on. Opening my eyes I look over Jack's shoulder and see Joe on the couch, his bloodshot slits for eyes staring, his mouth slightly open, still holding his beer but not drinking it. He's frozen. *Am I not sexy enough?* Insecurity weighs down like an anvil on my chest; Is Jack disappointed because I can't lure Joe towards us? I wish that Jack would blindfold me so I wouldn't have to look at Joe again.

Jack puts his hand up my top and starts to squeeze my tit. "Please don't pull my shirt off," I beg him in a whisper. He knows I'm embarrassed about my small boobs. I don't want him to reveal them to Joe.

"Shhh," he whispers as he uses both hands to pull my shirt up. He lays my shirt over my face and I am grateful to have my eyes covered. I arch my back to make my boobs look bigger and my stomach more flat. Wrapping my forearms across my eyes and forehead, holding the cloth to my face, now I can't see Joe's disappointment in me. I will focus on how good it feels for Jack to touch me. He kisses my breasts, my ribs, my stomach. I moan loudly and wonder why Joe hasn't joined us. Why won't he fool around with me? Then, I don't feel anything. No one is touching me. I don't want to look, I don't want to lift the shirt off and face reality. Maybe Tricia walked in? Maybe Joe walked out? Maybe

Jack walked out?

I feel hands untying my shoes. I let out a loud sigh so Jack knows I'm relieved. I'm no longer capable of speaking in words. Only moans, gasps, and eventually, hopefully, screams. When Jack gets my shoes and socks off he rubs my feet for a minute and then kisses my toes. He nibbles on the end of my big toe and then licks it. I steal a peek at Jack's face; he is looking right at Joe as he sticks my big toe in his mouth. He sucks on it like a Popsicle, wrapping his tongue around and using suction as he goes up. He pulls my toe from his mouth and yells toward the living room "Come on in here and maybe she'll suck your dick like that." He puts my foot against his hard dick and I can feel the heat coming through his jeans. Jack crawls up the side of me and unbuttons my skirt; once that's gone there's nothing left but my white cotton panties.

I don't want to hear the half-hearted protest Joe is mumbling from the other room. I re-cover my eyes and wrap my arms tighter across my head. I want Joe to be a willing participant. Jack lies beside me, caressing me, kissing me. He seems to be touching me everywhere but inside my panties which is making me more desperate for him to. Every touch is more intense because I can't see it coming and I know someone else can.

"Please fuck me," I beg Jack.

"I will if Joe will." Jack says to me, "You have to beg Joe."

"But he doesn't want to." I'm rejected by both of them now.

"Of course he does, he's dying to. I thought you wanted to make Joe happy."

"I do, but I want him to want me."

"Tell Joe you want him to fuck you," Jack says. "Just say it."

"Joe," I whisper from behind the T-shirt, "please fuck me." I shouldn't have to tell him, he should be dying to.

Iggy Pop is singing my life through the speakers:

♫ Well, I'm losing all my feelings
And I'm running out of friends
You know you lied to me in the beginning
Baby now you're gonna try to bring me
Try to bring me to the end
I need somebody, baby
I need somebody too
I need somebody, baby
Just like you, just like you, just like you ♫

"Say it again so he can hear." Jack pulls the T-shirt away from my face and strokes my hair.

"Joe, please, please, come fuck me," I say as I look into Jack's eyes.

Jack smiles as his hand finally reaches down into my panties. My hips writhe against his hand, but he still holds out. I tuck my face into his neck. It aches so badly between my legs; I know what boys mean when they call it blue balls. I hold onto Jack with both my arms, hugging him tightly. He hugs me back, rolling us onto our sides. He's finally going to make love to me.

Then, I feel Joe lie down behind me. Cold hands grab my panties and pull them off of me. Without so much as a kiss, Joe sticks his dick in me and starts to hump. Jack is in front of me and holding me, asking, "Do you like that baby?"

"Yeah," I answer, because that's what I'm supposed to say.

I open my eyes and look around the room. Sunlight comes through the windows. It might be beautiful, if I wasn't wondering why I'm lying here in the middle of the day. Not sure why I'm paying more attention to detail now, with this stranger's dick inside me, but now I notice this mattress is on the floor. I see the dresser has half the drawer pulls missing and it sits lopsided on stained carpet. There isn't any other furniture in this room, Joe certainly doesn't have anything nice. I expect to have so much more when *I'm* 28 years old. I watch the dust floating through the air in the sunlight, and I remember as a child I used to think those were all tiny little worlds, like in the Dr. Seuss book "*Horton Hears a Who*". I close my eyes again, and bury my face as hard as I can into Jack's neck and hold him tight. This isn't at all like I'd hoped. Joe's not here to please me. It's like he's not even aware I'm here at all. He may as well be jacking off; my body is no more than a giant hand to him. I can tell by Joe's movements this will all be over in a minute.

I think about the nurses at the clinic, telling me to abstain from sex for at least two weeks because I am much more likely to get an infection now. Between the three of us in this room, it's probably me that cares the least.

I'll get what I deserve.

When Joe's done, he rolls over onto his back and I feel so very alone. Why do I hear myself begging Jack to fuck me when I am on a bed flanked by two men? I want to feel loved and adored. I want to feel like my pleasure matters. I've been waiting for hours and let down repeatedly. Joe forgot about me the minute he stuck his dick in. I thought grown men were supposed to be better lovers. Thirty minutes ago he was concerned with my homework load. Now, he is staring at the ceiling covered in sweat, lying next to me but a thousand miles away. How could this have been so different in my mind?

Jack pushes me onto my back and crawls on top of me, sticking his dick inside. He starts fucking me like Joe did, like he's using my body, completely unconcerned with my pleasure. Jack has never screwed me like this before. It's as if he is punishing me or intentionally making me feel like I don't matter. I squeeze my eyes shut but tears leak out. I want Jack to finish and get off me. I have to leave the room before they see me cry. I run my hands up and down and Jack's back, grab his ass and moan. I tell him how fat his cock feels compared to Joe's, hoping that'll help him cum quicker so he can get off me and hoping it might hurt Joe's ego. Jack rolls onto his back on the other side of me, each of them spent, useless.

I get up and leave the two of them there, naked on the bed, limp. I walk to the bathroom, to the dirty, moldy shower. I'm glad the old pipes make noise so those boys can't hear me cry. I let the brown rusty water flow down the drain 'til it runs clear. I stay in the shower until the warm water runs out, using as much of Tricia's toiletries as I want. When I get out, I search the bathroom cabinets and treat myself to a fresh clean towel, and a few drops of baby oil to smooth my hair.

I have not overstayed my welcome. They owe me.

21 • WILD IN THE STREETS

When I get out of the shower Joe and Jack are fully clothed sitting back on the couch. They're talking quietly and they sound serious.

"Grab your shit, K.P., we have to go," Jack demands.

"What, are you kidding me? What did I do?"

"Your dad came by here and yelled at me and Joe."

"Yeah, he insisted he was going to bust into my house and drag you out of the shower. I had to convince him it was Tricia in there," Joe says, "Your dad said if he finds out you're here, he'll call the police and tell them I'm harboring a runaway or I've kidnapped you. Obviously you're going to have to go."

Sitting on the couch, Joe looks younger and more scared than Jack. I can't believe I thought this guy was a man.

"I told your dad I thought you were at Tammy's house, so he's probably headed over there," Jack says.

Great, the only friend I have at school to help me is Tammy, and now Jack sent my dad over there to yell at her.

"How does your dad know where my house is?" Joe asks.

"I don't know." It figures Joe is more concerned with himself than what's going to happen to me now. "Maybe he followed me when I came here after school?"

"And what, watched us through the windows for the past hour? You think he waited until you got in the shower to knock on the door?" Joe is pissed at *me*, as if I wanted my dad to show up here.

"If he was watching through the windows, he must have been whacking it," Jack volunteers a little hand demonstration with his comment.

"Can we go, Jack?" I sling my backpack over my shoulder.

"Good luck to you," Joe mumbles.

"Thanks for nothing," I say, not looking back.

Fuck him for acting all shy, like we're strangers who've just met and had tea, while I still have his cum dripping out of me. I know I'm nothing but a great story he will get to tell everyone he meets for years to come. To me he's nothing more than a bad memory that'll take years to forget. Stupid little pencil dick. "3-minute Joe." That's how I'll remember him.

As we walk down the driveway, I'm not even thinking about looking out for my dad, but Jack is.

"Why don't you walk off ahead to the sidewalk and if he grabs you, I'll pull him off of you so you can run? If I go first, he'll beat the crap out of me and get you anyway."

This conversation reminds me of the phrase: *Know Your Enemy*. This is the streetwise stuff that I still need to learn. I walk slowly to the sidewalk while Jack lingers behind. Looking up and down the street, I wonder if my dad will come back here once he discovers I'm not at Tammy's house. My dad never invested this much time in me when I lived at home, unless I was in trouble; he could spend hours yelling at me, inventing rules, devising punishments that he was never around to enforce in the days that followed.

I don't see my dad anywhere, so I turn to look at Jack and give him the okay sign.

"Now what?" I ask Jack, feeling defeated. I'm free to walk along the sidewalk, big deal, big accomplishment. I still don't have a plan.

It's dusk as we take off walking towards the Redondo Beach pier. We can't seem to go more than a block without running into someone Jack knows. By the time we get to the pier there's a group of six of us. We all sport torn jeans and high-tops or engineer boots, flannel shirts tied around our waists and T-shirts creatively adorned with our band allegiance. I wear a Mickey Mouse T-shirt that I got in a thrift store and I've put a bullet hole in his forehead with black marker and red blood dripping down the center of his smiling face.

At the pier there are families out for the evening, kids eating corndogs, churros, and chocolate dipped ice cream cones. The men have mustaches and longish hair. Ten years ago this was the symbol of rebellion, now the look of a family man. Somehow my buddies' buzz cuts have become the more threatening image. It used to be you couldn't get into school without one.

It's fun to walk around as a group and be gawked at. We bug our eyes out at people that look at us for too long or flip off people that point at us. I'm finally part of a family. I feel tough, invincible; I now have control over what people see in me. It is no longer up to them how I am viewed.

We don't have any money. There is no kindness handed to our group. We are the villains. The pier police know our role and ride their bikes by us more often than the other families here.

When the group of us walks into a big clean women's bathroom above the main part of the pier, I whisper my bright idea to Jack,

"We can come here to sleep if no one will take us in."

"People fucking love me; we are NEVER going to be without roommates." Jack says loudly. "This place sucks!" Then more quietly, to me, he says, "They lock the doors at night anyway." Ripping the paper towel dispenser from the wall as he says this, every paper towel in there is now wide brown confetti in the air fluttering to the floor.

Everyone joins in to beat up this bathroom, kicking and smashing anything we can. Someone knocks a trashcan down, spreading its contents across the floor. It sounds like an industrial gong as it's smashed and transformed from a cylinder to a flat metal strip. The next paper towel dispenser comes down, raining more lunch bag colored confetti. I grab the other trashcan and dump it upside down, feeling empowered yet conflicted. Moments ago I thought this bathroom could have served as an overnight home. I'm sad that I need such a home and mad that I could be locked out of it. This external chaos is still so much better than the internal subversive shit at home.

The rampage and destruction is loud and exciting. If this were a movie, "Wild in the Streets" by the Circle Jerks would be the soundtrack. It lasts only minutes before we know we have to run fast to make sure we don't get caught. To be dressed like us and running is an admission of guilt in the eyes of adults. I look back as the door closes on its slow hinge; that bathroom is no longer disguised as a safe place.

Next we head to Kim's house, a ten minute walk from the pier up the street. She is nice to me and doesn't seem interested in sleeping with Jack. I don't know where her parents are, but there are always a lot of kids hanging at her house. Kim lets me borrow a pair of pants so I can put the clothes in my backpack in her washer. I'm grateful.

A crowd of kids fills the den at the back of the house. The dim light reveals dark walls covered in wood and a sliding glass door. There is a couch and coffee table next to an open tile area. Everyone is drinking beer, and I take one, happy to be part of the group. Jack, of course, drinks much faster than the rest of us. The "Hell Comes to Your House" record is playing and when "Lude Boy" by Social Distortion plays, the guys start slamming in the open space. I sit on the couch and lean over the back to watch them. It looks like fun and I want to join in. I'm not certain Jack will approve and he's pretty wasted already. The slamming is gaining momentum. The power and energy are increasing, like a magic circle in a coven, or an Indian fire dance. Jack jumps over the couch mimicking a stage dive and crashes into the coffee table, spilling drinks and shattering glass everywhere. The song ends, a dramatic silence descends, everyone stares at him to see what will happen next.

The next song, "Telling Them," by Social D. begins; the perfect soundtrack. The high-pitched guitar is poking my nerves repeatedly, incessantly, like a bully's finger. Jack looks at me like he wants me to beg, and I foolishly take the bait.

"Dammit, Jack! Please don't cut yourself. Come on, have another drink."

I know it is pointless. The scene is too perfect. He holds half the room's breath hostage. His shirt is off, booze and sweat on his beautiful, masculine body. Broken glass litters the carpet at his feet like an offering of precious stones. There is already a little bit of blood dotting his flesh, accenting where his skin was pierced as the cups and bottles broke against him. Jack, our savior, preparing himself to be sacrificed.

"Please don't cut yourself," I beg.

The lyrics start to shout and it's as if they were written for this moment:

> ♫ I love the sound when I smash the glass,
> If I get caught they're gonna kick my ass.
> My mommy's worried about the way I drink,
> My daddy can't figure out the way I think. ♫

The glass glimmers in the light. He picks up a shard and pushes it into his brown Italian skin and opens it to red. He is euphoric, loving the attention and the pain. He cuts again, across his chest, like war paint ready for battle against the world. I feel like he is against me.

"God dammit Jack!"

I slap his face and he looks pained from my disappointment in him, not his self-inflicted wounds. The pain in his eyes doesn't halt my mouth. I am already yelling at him.

"You ASSHOLE! Why did you do that? You said you only did that when you were unhappy." His eyes begin to flick with anger; I've embarrassed him by interrupting his moment, and betrayed him by reprimanding him in front of everyone.

Jack storms out of the room. I hear the front door slam. Everyone is silent, only the sound of the music playing in the background fills the air. I'm filled with regret, wearing a stranger's clothes, in the home of a person I've only just met. Everyone stares at me like I shot down Superman.

I run out of the front door and into the dark. I'm not sure where I am. So high on adrenaline from smashing the bathroom, I didn't pay attention to where Kim's house is. I simply followed Jack here, like one of his sheep. I've had just enough to drink to confuse myself, but not enough to avoid being accountable.

Seeing a few drops of blood on the ground, I try to follow, but the trail ends by the next house. I don't know what to do. I call out his name, but not loud enough to alert the neighbors. Any second he will hop out and either hug me or hit me. Either way is fine, but I don't want him to leave me.

Speaking into the darkness; "Jack, please come back." But he's gone.

I go back and knock on Kim's door. "Has he come back yet?"

"No, but your pants are dry."

I go in and change clothes. My clean black Levi's feel good against my skin, even when the buttons burn me. I fold up the clothes Kim loaned me and apologize for creating a scene that caused her party to end. The crowd has left.

"Why did you yell at him? He always does that, and YOU do too!" She points to the scars on my arm and I pull down the sleeve of my sweatshirt. I feel like she's defending his right to cut himself, but blaming me.

"I only do it when I'm mad, or sad. I'm happy with him so I have no reason to hurt myself. He said he was happy with me. He said he would stop."

"You can't change him. He's been this way for a long time. You can crash here tonight if you want. He might come back."

Kim gives me a pillow, a blanket and a beer. The den is a mess and the perfect setting for my life. I wonder what would make me more welcome, cleaning up or staying quiet. I think about Jack out there with no shirt on, bleeding, drunk. Is he alone and sad? Is he already at someone else's house partying? Is he already in another girl's bed? I can't stand the thought of Jack not loving me. I don't know where I'll go if he's not back in the morning when I wake up. I drink my beer quickly but it doesn't take the pain away.

The beginning of that song, "Reject Yourself" by 100 Flowers goes through my head. The way the guitar starts off slowly and then increasingly becomes more manic. I whisper the lyrics to myself...

♫ Reject yourself,
Reject yourself
and your family of ideals.♫

I reach down on the ground and pick up one of the pieces of broken glass, his broken glass. This is his fault; later we'll heal together. I pull the blanket up over my head and push up the sleeve on my arm. I push all my beaded swivel bracelets towards my hand, exposing light scars and scabs from old cuts. Most of my mind is saying, *don't do this, this isn't right. You will regret this, this won't fix anything.*

But there is a voice inside me getting louder, screaming, *I want to control my pain, not them. I hate everyone, most of all myself. I pushed Jack away when he was all I had.* I push the glass onto my skin harder and harder until it finally breaks through. There is a welcome rush of heat, a distraction. I pull the glass edge harder across and the skin on my arm opens up to pink and then red. I can't feel anything but this. I don't want to feel anything but this. The next cut is easier, like a second mile of skating or the second cigarette, an effective, euphoric habit.

22 • RELEASED

Jack comes around school the next day and visits me at lunch like he did the day we met. This time he hops the fence, and when he lands on my side of the fence, all anger and loneliness I felt waking up this morning without him next to me have been dispelled. Tammy and our few friends create a half-circle to conceal him from Mr. H, who has playground duty and can't see anything but how nicely his teenaged plaything is developing.

"Where did you go last night?" I ask, trying not to sound jealous or accusing.

"The cops saw me running down the street and picked me up."

"Oh shit!"

"Yeah, but it's okay," Jack says, "They made me empty my pockets to make sure I didn't rob anyone. Then they drove me home and made my mom promise to keep me in for the night. Where did you stay?"

"Kim let me stay at her house."

"That's good. Kim's cool."

"Yeah, she was nice to me," I tell him. But Jack is used to everyone being nice to him. I don't think he understands what it's like for the rest of the world. I live my life under the assumption that everyone hates me.

The end of lunch arrives too soon and I don't want to say goodbye. I contemplate hopping the fence with him and leaving. I could walk right out of the front doors and no one would stop me. Somehow, I have managed to stay in school for three weeks without living with my parents. If I ditch, someone from school will call my parents and then they will quit paying the tuition. I need to have somewhere to go. As much as I hate to part ways with Jack, he hops the fence and I go back inside. I'm glad I can keep up with all my schoolwork during class. It would be impossible to get any work done once I left the school grounds.

Twenty minutes before the dismissal bell, my teacher tells me to go to the principal's office. I can't imagine what I've done wrong. I have four skirts that I leave around at people's houses, giving me a week's worth of uniforms. Once I got rid of that initial bag of speed, I didn't sell anymore, figured I'd quit while I was ahead. I wish there was a big long hallway to walk down so I had time to think, to devise a plan or an argument for whatever the Principal was about to accuse me of.

The administration office is right next door to my classroom, so I walk out one door and right into the next. I stand in front of the chest-high counter and tell the secretary, "I'm here to see the principal."

"She's waiting for you. Go on in." The secretary usually has a big smile, to go with her big brown hair and puffy body. Now, her eyes looked sad, disappointed. I can't imagine what she thinks I've done but I'm certain of my innocence.

"Hi Mrs. Mitchell, you wanted to see me?" I stand terrified before this small, ancient woman.

"Please sit down, Karen."

I avoid her eyes and look to the most talked about item in her office instead. Hung on a nail from a leather loop is a big wooden paddle with holes drilled in it and the words "The Board of Education" painted across.

"Why are there holes drilled in the paddle?" I ask.

"Less wind resistance," she says with a smirk.

"Huh," is all I can say to that. "Did I do something wrong?"

"It has come to my attention that you are not living with your parents. Is this true?"

"Where did you hear that?"

"I asked you a question. Is this true?" Mrs. Mitchell is all business.

"Well, yes. But….."

"You can't attend school here if you are not living with your parents."

"Why not? My parents paid my tuition, didn't they?"

"You are not a good example for the other students here."

"What do you mean? I'm not living with my parents and I choose to stay in school. I'm still passing my classes. So how am I not a good influence?"

I see my friends passing the office window on their way out of school. For them, the pressure has just ended for the day.

"I see you smoking cigarettes across the street with those weird

kids. You are looking more bizarre every week. Orange-ish hair, a stack
of earrings! Who wears purple basketball shoes with dresses? Your
grades may be passing, but are now Cs instead of As, and I presume
they will continue to decline." With each sentence, it's like Mrs. Mitchell
is unfolding a piece of paper, but I stubbornly refuse to see each tiny
note she shows me.

"Cs are passing; I swear I'll bring my grades back up. I hang out
with the same friends I've always had in school; I am the same student
no matter where I live. I promise to do better." I stare at her shoes.
They are blue and white wingtip style pumps, the perfect New Wave
shoes that make her kind of a hypocrite in regards to appearance. Mrs.
Mitchell, the ancient New-Waver. I will not look at her face. If I don't
cry maybe she won't tell me what I don't want to hear.

"The Bible says you are to honor your father and your mother
and if you are a runaway, you are not following one of the Ten
Commandments. I can't allow you to attend school here any longer."
Shit! There it is. The paper is finally unfolded completely and she has
held up the big sign that says: YOU DON'T GET TO STAY IN
SCHOOL.

How am I supposed to argue with the Bible? My eyes burn with
the tears I don't want her to see. Time for me to walk out.

"Sit down, Karen," she says. Her old voice is frail and shaky,
but somehow she still seems bigger than me.

"Why? Are my parents coming?" A tornado spins inside me.
Anger, fear and sadness mesh together in an ugly dark cloud above my
head. Maybe my parents are going to grab me from here; I've been set
up.

"I'd like you to stay until all your classmates have gone, so as
not to cause a ruckus."

"They aren't my classmates now, and you aren't my principal
anymore." She wants to control me, but not help me; like she is holding
onto my hands but kicking me away with her feet. Time for me to get
out of here in case the police or my parents are on their way. *"Know your
enemy,"* I tell myself again.

Not turning my head as I leave, I tell her, "I could have
honored my father and mother by staying in school. YOU forced me to
be a dropout." Why did I even say that? I don't expect her to care.

Another door closes behind me.

At the sidewalk Tammy and Jack wait for me. Tammy hands me
a sandwich bag full of quarters. She steals money from the apartment
washing machines because her mom is the manager and Tammy knows
where the keys are.

"There's probably fifteen dollars in there, enough for hair dye,"

Tammy says. I guess everybody knew I wouldn't get to stay in school but me. Somehow I know my mom is the force behind this new development. The next time she sees me, I will have awesome hair.

Walking away from school, I'm not tethered to anything or anyone but Jack now. From here on out we can only move forward together.

We meet up with some friends who are headed uptown. Many of them are my age and their parents let them go to Hollywood on the weekends and dress however they want. Not Tammy, though; her mom will only let her look pretty, or sexy. There is no chance in hell she would let Tammy look like a punk. Tammy takes off and walks the rest of the way home alone. Jack and I decide Hollywood is the place to be and take our baggy of quarters on the road. Why not? I am ready to have an adventure and my parents won't find me there.

Seven of us pile into a Dodge Dart, three in front and four in back. We drive to a show we probably can't get into, knowing that standing outside the gig will still be fun. Once outside the show I see that everyone is cooler than me. Girls wear dresses with fishnets or torn black tights; they know how to do makeup and wear high heels. I look like a boy with my black jeans and purple high tops. I need better hair, better shoes. I covet the look of fishnets and engineer boots.

I've tried on engineer boots once and they made me feel like stomping around, like I could kick anyone's butt. Boots make you feel something when you wear them, like therapeutic footwear...When you put a little kid in rain boots or cowboy boots for the first time they start stomping around like they are ready to take on the world. When I was little girl, I remember wanting construction boots like my dad. My parents finally gave in and bought them for me. I wore them to school one time, got teased, never wore them again. Another time my dad took me shoe shopping and I picked out these cool knee-high shiny red boots with a tiny heel.

"Why are you dressing her up like a Go-go dancer?" My mom was angry and made us take them back. I felt awesome in them, like Wonder Woman.

Engineer boots cost seventy or eighty dollars, so there is no chance my parents would have put any money towards them. If I paid for them myself and brought them home, they would've thrown them away.

Hair is the biggest indicator of a person's commitment to the scene. Using Sun-in to make my hair look orange is something I did secretly. My parents think changing my hair color makes me an entirely different person, even though my mom has been dying her hair since she was 18. I guess they hate the idea of me coloring my hair because I wouldn't be able to take my hair off and hide if they needed to introduce me to one of their business colleagues.

The music gushing through the club's back door brings my thoughts back to my immediate surroundings. Steam rises from sweaty bodies as they exit. The walls throb with bass and drums like a pulse that is keeping me alive.

When the gig ends, I am amazed at how many people were in the club. Like a clown car, more and more keep piling out. A few cop cars are parked across the street; officers watch from inside their cars while kids wander around talking, smoking, some of them drinking beers. After about 30 minutes, the police got out of their cars.

"Okay, kids. Time to go home!" a cop says over a bullhorn.

"Fuck off!" Kids yell, flipping off the cops.

"This is your last warning," the bullhorn announces. Who would take them seriously? There are way more of us than them.

Down the street in the distance I see the outline of four-legged giants in the fog. The giants are moving closer, a rhythmic, plastic, crashing sound getting louder. Eventually I see that the noisy giants are actually cops on horses. I've never seen that before except on T.V. Where do they keep horses in Los Angeles? There are no fields or meadows here. Cops that aren't on horses walk in front holding transparent, plastic shields, like medieval warriors. The cops beat their shields with billy clubs. That's what that sound was, the rhythm of the cops getting ready to beat up on the kids.

"Can we go wait at the car for our ride?" I ask Jack.

"Yeah, come on," he says as he picks up a beer bottle from the ground and launches it towards the cops.

We left one person behind in Hollywood. I'm glad it wasn't me. The backseat is less crowded, and every time we go over a bump the car bounces up and down like one of those quarter rides in front of the grocery store. This car, like my whole life, seems to be held together with rusty nails and duct tape. I don't know how drunk our driver is, but in addition to bobbing vertically, the car seems to be wiggling horizontally all over the lane. Even though the streets are less crowded, the ride home seems way more dangerous.

I'm relieved when we get back to Redondo Beach, grateful that Kim's back door is unlocked and we have a place to crash. I tiptoe in as quietly as I can. Jack saunters in like a drunken cowboy, his boots and leather jacket making a spanking noise against the fake leather couch. I pull his boots off for him, and then unlace my high-tops and lie on the couch. It's pointless trying to snuggle tonight, Jack reeks of beer and sweat and is already passed out. I turn around and lie with my head at Jack's feet to give myself more room. Panic starts in my body and breaks into my mind. Shouldn't I call someone to tell them we made it back safely? If something would've happened to me in Hollywood on the ride home, no one would've known. Staring at the ceiling, the deafening silence makes me feel like I'm lost in space.

In the morning, I phone my parents. I want them to care about where I am, to be connected to them, just not suffocated by them. Jack rolls his eyes at me. He has his mom trained and can do whatever he wants, come and go as he pleases. I want to get to that point with my parents, but I doubt it will ever happen. They want total control over me.

"I loved walking through the mall with you. People would turn their heads because you were beautiful," Mom says through the phone. "Now people stare because you look so weird. Why do you want this negative attention?"

"I like the way I look now. Why does it matter? Why is it so important? Why can't you love me if I don't have feathered hair? You used to ask me why I had to look like everyone else, so you wouldn't have to buy me fifty dollar jeans. Now you want me to look like everyone else."

"Your outward appearance is an expression of your inner turmoil. It's an indication of a greater problem deep inside you," she says.

"Mom, maybe my inner turmoil is because you are judging me on my appearance. I can be a good kid, get good grades, get along with everyone and still look the way I want to look. I am fine. You guys are the ones making a big deal about clothes and music. I can't win."

"I'm not going to agree to let you look cheap and easy or weird. You are begging for negative attention when you look like that, and Jack is the most negative of all."

"I love you Mom, talk to you soon," I say hanging up on her.

I turn to Jack, "Fuck it. Let's do my hair, she doesn't ever want me back."

23 ● FLUFFY

We meet up with Brenda, a friend of Jack's. She has bleach at home and needs to "do her roots". I didn't know that I'd have to re-dye my hair every month, but I think it's worth it, I've always wanted to have platinum hair, one of the things my parents refused no matter how I negotiated. When we get to her house, I'm surprised to see that Brenda's mom is home and there to help us with this process.

"Want some cookies? We made them last night," her mom offers, as she sets up chemicals and mixing bowls on top of their dining room table.

I bite into a cookie and wonder, Am I the only one whose parents can't love her if she doesn't look like them? Of course, this reinforces my desire to be as different from them as possible.

The bleach is thick and frothy and doesn't look anything like the stuff my mom uses to dye her hair. Once on my head, the froth creeps onto and scorches my scalp. I never expected this to hurt, the chemicals are so strong. When we wash the bleach out, my hair is Ronald Mc Donald orange.

"I look like a clown," I cry. Maybe Brenda and her mom don't know what they are doing?

"You need to do it a second time," Brenda says.

"Do it again?" I'm confused. "It's going to hurt like hell!"

"This time it will turn white, I promise. If you don't like the way it looks, it will be light enough to dye it blue or whatever." The thought of purple hair to match my purple high tops is a happy thought, but mainly I don't want to leave the house with lame hair.

The burning isn't nearly as severe. I sit tense and worried that I am going to be bald when we're done, and not in a cool "I shaved my head" kind of way. When I bend with my head in the sink, conditioner spiraling down the drain, I pray in my head, *"I don't want to regret this. Please let me look good, please let me have hair."*

Brenda wraps a towel around my head and I sit back down at the kitchen table. As I pull the towel off, all eyes are on me, to see what has become of our kitchen science experiment.

"Wow! You look like Blondie!"

"Yeah you look like Debbie Harry!"

"Baby, you look hot."

Brenda hands me a mirror. My hair bright white, platinum; finally something has changed and I've been transformed.

"Let's take a bus to Hollywood!" I suggest, wanting to do something monumental.

"I told Tricia we would help her at the Laundromat, she's going to give us movie passes and beer."

Why do I still have people telling me what to do? If I am free, why am I pushed to rebel?

"Thank you for doing my hair, for making me feel like a movie star. Brenda is lucky to have a mom that loves and accepts her; I wish I had a mom like you." I give them both a hug and follow Jack out the door.

"I've always thought it was odd that Laundromat has to be capitalized, but love and lust don't," I say to Jack.

"So what?" Jack answers.

I guess he doesn't understand the significance of what I am trying to say, What I'm saying probably isn't significant.

I've never been in a Laundromat before, having always had a washer and dryer at home. The dryers are huge; you can easily fit several loads of laundry or even a small person inside one. We climb into the baskets with wheels. The sides are low, making them easier to get into than shopping carts. We race them along the floor next to the smooth counters, which are long enough for us to lie on end to end. I like the vending machine with the tiny boxes of laundry soap, especially the detergent called Cheer. I imagine buying a box and soaking in Cheer, making my whole day exceptional.

Drinking a beer Tricia brought, I'm ready for it to baptize others sins against me away.

"Drink it faster or you won't feel anything." Jack says.

I try to gulp it down, but it tastes like dirty socks washed in carbonated water, the liquid wrung into an ugly brown bottle.

Tricia does people's laundry for money. I'm impressed with this idea and decide I'll do it when I get older. If you have to do your laundry anyway, why not get paid for your time? I think it's smart and resourceful. She usually has Jack or another friend help her fold.

"Doing someone else's laundry is called Fluff and Fold," Tricia says. This is hilarious to me, but it could be that drinking is adding to the humor.

"We are going to play the matching game," Tricia says as she dumps a pile of clean, dry socks in front of us. We race to match up the socks and fold the pairs into each other. Whoever has the biggest pile of completed socks gets to decide what to do with the next beer. Jack, of course, is winning, because he has played this game before. He knows how to cheat, hiding a handful of socks so it is impossible for anyone but him to match them. "You lose! You have to drink my beer. I'm gonna get you fucked up."

"I can't drink anymore, I'm feeling sick."

"You're such a lightweight," he teases.

"I already drank a beer in like two minutes! YOU drink this one!" I give Jack the bottle to make our intoxication even, but it still won't even be close.

"If you don't drink your beer I'm going to fluff and fold you," he says.

"Huh? Fluffy what?"

We're laughing uncontrollably,

"Mellow out!" Tricia says, sounding like a mom. "Quiet down!"

"Yep, I'm gonna fluff and fold you!" Jack proclaims as he picks me up and starts to stuff me into the dryer.

"No! NO! I'm gonna be sick! You're gonna make me throw up!"

"Brace yourself. Put your arms and legs out wide, like you're doing a cart wheel. It'll be fun!"

"God dammit, Jack! Knock it off! If you get me kicked out of another Laundromat, I'm gonna kick your ass!" Tricia seems almost stern. Her voice is serious, but this is the first time I've seen her really smile.

I'm giggling way too hard to fight Jack off, he's bigger and stronger, I'm drunk, woozy and a little afraid. We wrestle each other against the open dryer door. We are laughing, sure, but seriously I do not want to go in there. He isn't letting up and before I can get the upper hand, I am closed inside. It's hot and muffled in here. I'm unable to hear what Jack says from the other side of the glass, as he motions for me to hold on. His hand goes up out of view and he turns the dryer on.

I'm drunk and clumsy inside the dryer. I do my best to brace myself like he said, by putting myself into a cartwheel position. My arms are already weak from fighting against him. There is nothing graceful about my dryer cartwheel, my head bashes and bonks around against the sides. Spinning around in the dryer a few turns, the heat starts to build. The space feels too small, and it seems urgent that I escape. Moving my hand, I try to push the door open from the inside. Letting go causes me to fall from the top to the bottom of the dryer and go around again. I position my limbs like a starfish to brace myself again, but then lose my grip and kick myself in the nose with my own knee. The glass between us starts to cloud with moisture. The dryer smells of beer, but perhaps I'm imagining that in my drunken, spinning state. The beer churns in my stomach, bubbles like a stinking rancid acid in my throat and comes out through my nose. My face is wet with tears, snot and bile when finally I manage to kick the door open. Cool air and their maniacal laughter flood into my hot, budget carnival ride from hell.

"You looked like a Raggedy Ann doll, like you didn't even have any bones." Tricia doesn't try to hide her amusement of my stupidity.

"Oh my God! You didn't even try to brace yourself!" Jack doesn't seem to care that I'm hurt.

"Jack, your little Blondie looks like she's about to cry," Tricia warns him.

"Shut up, Tricia. K.P. is tough, she can handle it." I'm proud that Jack is defending me. As he puts his arm around me, I've already forgiven him for stuffing me in the dryer. It's me and him against Tricia now.

"Yeah, I'm super fluffy right now," I tell them as I light up a cigarette and start to walk outside.

"You guys carry these two bags back to my house and I'll get the rest," Tricia says. "I'll make some Stove Top stuffing for dinner when I'm done." I guess Joe didn't tell her about my dad coming by her house, or, like me, she assumes my dad won't be back a second time. I would be happy if I never saw Joe again in my life.

"Stuffing! I'm staying!" Jack quotes the Stove Top commercial as he hands me a black garbage bag full of clean clothes to carry. I've never had Stove Top before, but I certainly feel like I've earned my dinner.

We drop off the bags of clothes, then walk the two blocks from Tricia's house down to the beach. I am fourteen years old, lived here my whole life, but have never been to the beach after dark.

At night, the beach is entirely different; looking off into the horizon is like looking into outer space—dark, empty, endless. We leave our shoes on the cement Strand; stepping onto the sand feels like we've stepped on the moon. The sand is freezing against my bare feet, aching so deep as if my bones are being crushed. The sand is damp and sticks to my feet annoyingly, not warm and soothing like when I was a twelve year old at the beach playing volleyball. As we get closer to the shore, pounding waves create a salty cold mist that hangs heavy in the air, leaving my face and arms sticky.

The ocean sounds like static, rumbles like an earthquake, rolling closer like it is going to consume me. Even though no one else is around, we have to yell to hear each other over the noise of the waves. Movie scenes come to mind where shoreline lovemaking is conveyed as romantic and beautiful. I imagine dirty wet sand on my back, against my ass, in places that will start to respond like sand paper.

My newly bleached hair is light and fluffy, lifted by the wind until it's tacky, tangled. The mess of it forms into a big white globe. A sticky bulb of chemically damaged fluff around my face, like I stuck my finger in a light socket, or my head itself is a light bulb. I'm the universal image of a "big idea" wandering around the moonlit beach, searching for a way to have basic needs met.

I want to be warm and dry.

I want to be fluffy.

24 ● CITADEL

"Let's go visit my friend Deborah," Jack says, pointing to the building named The Holiday Rivera towering above us. From the street it looks simple and logically laid out, but once we go through the doors in the center, it's like a giant labyrinth: six stories high— every floor is another maze. There must be three hundred apartments in here. I don't know how Jack can find his way around, but I know if we get into his friend's apartment, my parents could never find me.

After an elevator ride, more doors and hallways, Jack begins to hum the intro to the T.V. show "Get Smart". We are giggling when he knocks on a door that is answered by a woman who could be his aunt, with her olive skin and green eyes.

"Hey there, kiddo!" She gives Jack a big hug and then hugs me as she says, "Hi, I'm Deborah, come on in. What've you been up to, Jack?"

Deborah has thick, curly hair, that's feathered off her face. She wears a button up shirt with more buttons undone than my mom would approve of.

They talk like old friends. As usual, I don't know how to insert myself into the conversation, so I stand there like a dork. Jack's flirty with her like he is with everybody. She makes an effort to make me comfortable, so I wonder if she's trying to hide something or get something from me, but I always feel that way, especially with girls that Jack knows.

"So what's the story Jack? Are you looking for pot? Did you run away from home again?" I like how she gets straight to the point.

"No, but K.P. did," Jack tells her.

"Why's that, so you could spend more time with him, or so you don't have to go to school?"

127

"No, I went to school until they kicked me out. I'd go to school tomorrow if they'd let me."

"Really?" She says, surprised. "Why did you get kicked out?"

"They said I was a bad influence on the other kids."

"Were you?"

"I was still going to school, even though I wasn't living at home. If you ask me, I think that is a good influence."

"Ha! I think you're right about that. You kids want pizza? I was about to order one. My roommate isn't coming home tonight."

"Yes!" Jack and I say in unison.

We follow Deborah into the living room; her tan leather blazer and Le-Sportsac purse hang over the arm of the soft burgundy velvet couch. Where does Jack find these people? Deborah looks normal, like she could work at a bank or something.

"What does Deborah do that she can afford to live on the beach?" I ask Jack while she orders pizza.

"She works in an office as an artist or something," Jack says.

"What do you mean?" I've never heard of such a thing. I know nothing of artist jobs. Artists aren't respected in my family. When I was six, I told my mom I wanted to be an artist and her response was, "You can't be an artist, you don't even know how to draw." Now I'm told there is a job where you can be an *artist* who works in an *office* and be paid enough to live right across from the beach?

"I don't know what she does. She's never taken me to work with her," Jack says sarcastically.

"How did you meet Deborah?" I'm still trying to figure out their relationship.

"Shit, I don't know. But her roommate is a real hippie with long hair and a beard and little round John Lennon glasses." Jack says, not answering my question about Deborah.

Once she is off the phone, Deborah joins us on the couch.

"Deborah, how old are you?" I ask.

"I'm 26. How old are you?"

"I'll be 15 in July"

"Oh, you're a Cancer. I usually get along with Cancers."

"Are your mom and dad married?" I get the sense that she is actually interested in what I say, so of course I want to tell her everything.

"Yeah, but they hate each other. They are two entirely different people, I have no idea how they ever got together."

"Do you have brothers and sisters?" she asks.

"I have a brother who's two years older and perfect. My parents would love it if I was like him."

"What makes him perfect? Because he's older? Because he's a boy?" She's really trying to figure this out.

"I don't know what it is that makes them like him more. He gets good grades and I got good grades. He ran for Student Council, so I ran for Student Council. He was always on every type of sports team and now I play volleyball. No matter what I do, he's better. He's the favorite. My parents don't like the way I look, they don't like the way I act, and they don't like the people I like. My brother's preppy and I'm a punk."

"But it's not only about the way you look, right? Do you and your brother get along?"

"He hasn't liked me since the day my parents brought me home from the hospital. When I started to cry, he told them, *'Give baby Karen a hotdog and put her to bed.'* I think he was upset when it wasn't as easy as that."

I'm retelling the story my mother wrote in my baby book, a baby book entry about how my brother hates me.

"So, what made you finally run away? It sounds like things have been bad for a while. Did somebody hurt you, or hit you or...." her voice trails off but I know she's trying to ask if anyone's touching me at home.

"They're all crazy. I don't want to live like that. I don't want to learn that." I don't know how to explain to Deborah how it was to live with my family, how unwelcome I felt in my home.

"What do you mean crazy?"

"Well, like when I was 12, I was listening to the Rolling Stones, Some Girls album. My dad overheard the lyrics, *'Black girls just want to get fucked all night... I just don't have that much jam'*. The next thing I heard was the needle scratching across the album. I found my dad in the kitchen at the stove with the album warped on the burner above the flame. My dad was laughing saying, *'Boy, that's a hot record.'* Everybody I know has that album."

Deborah and Jack laugh, and I get it. I laugh when I tell that story too, because it's a funny story to tell. But I tell them it's not funny if you're the kid whose dad is such a spaz that he can't say, 'you'll need to return that album to the person you borrowed it from. I won't allow that language in this house.' Instead, his first instinct is to attack me.

I try again to explain to Deborah what I'm talking about.

"The only thing they agree on is if I don't look different, act different, and have different friends, then they're gonna send me away to some kind of boarding school. They don't like me, they don't like each other, and they don't like themselves. I don't want to grow up to be like them, I don't want to live with them. You know that Joe Jackson song where he sings "*Take me away, take me away, I don't wanna be like that*".

Jack starts laughing at me. "Joe Jackson. So Punk Rock."

"Shut up, Jack," Deborah says, jumping to my defense, "It's probably the most punk rock thing either one of you has done all day"

"Are you on drugs?" Deborah asks me. "Are your parents mad because you are getting high with this guy?"

"I've been stoned once in my life when I was 12. I've been drunk twice in my life, once when I was 10 and once a few days ago in the Laundromat."

"Yeah, it took her a whole beer to get drunk," Jack volunteers.

"I got fluffy," I laugh.

"You got fluffy?" Deborah is confused.

"I stuffed her in the dryer." Jack is so proud of this. I reach up and touch the tender bruises on my head.

"You're such a dick, Jack," Deborah says as she gets up from the couch and goes into the kitchen. She comes back with a bag of those frosted animal cookies, the pink and white ones with the little specks of rainbow candy balls on them. I love those things.

"Okay here's the deal, you can stay here tonight. And as long as there's no problem with your parents, I'll try work it out with my roommate that you can stay here longer. I was on my own when I was young and I know how hard it is to do the right thing. If you start getting loaded, I'll kick you out. If you steal from me, I'll kick your ass."

I jump up from the chair and hug her as hard as I can. She is my new best friend. I let my tears of gratitude come. "Thank you, Deborah."

"I wish someone would have helped me when I was your age," Deborah says. "And I want to find a way for you to get back in school."

"I wish you were my mom."

"Well, I probably wouldn't be letting you date *him*," she says jokingly

"Fuck you, Deborah!" Jack says.

"I'm sure you mean, '*Thank you*', you dick." Deborah smiles at him and she pats me on the back letting me know it's time to stop hugging her already.

We eat cookies 'til the pizza comes, then devour all of the pizza as well. Living proof that dessert first won't spoil your appetite. In spite of having more to eat this evening than I've had in weeks, I feel lighter than ever. I have hope.

"I'll probably be gone to work when you guys wake up in the morning," Deborah says, handing us some blankets and pillows. "The top two shelves in the fridge are mine, and the top 2 shelves in the pantry are mine. Eat what you like, and leave the kitchen as you found it."

We kiss and cuddle into the night. I fall into the deepest most satisfying sleep I've had in the weeks I've been on the run.

When we wake up, the giant window throws beautiful diffused light into the room. I open the big doors wide, the ocean breeze is strong and cool. I can smell and taste the salt air, like we're right on the sand but it's not miserable like when we were there last night. I curl my toes into the carpet. This is the best of both worlds. It's nice to experience the elements, but still have protection from them.

Do people below look up and wonder how I arrived on a beach front balcony? I often ponder when passing by mansions, "*What does it take to end up here, to get a house on the beach?*" I imagine they would all have the same answers: "Be a doctor, be a lawyer, be somebody you're not." Or perhaps they might say "My parents gave me this house, it's been passed down for generations." But this is the era where parents get divorced, adult assets are divided and kids are left with nothing. The only thing passed down from generations these days is emotional baggage.

25 ● P.O.P.

Staying at Deborah's house is great. At night we sit on the balcony and eat dinner. I look below at the people lining up along the sidewalk watching the sunset, waiting for the legendary green flash that never comes. The sky turns from orange to purple and then slowly fades to black. The sidewalk clears as the people go home. I feel as if I am finally home. Deborah left home when she was young, but she never explained why. I don't feel right to press her for hard answers, but I can tell that's why she wants to help me.

I know eventually Deborah will get tired of the extra mouths to feed. I do my best to keep the apartment spotless and stay out of everyone's way. But I know as long as I'm not in school everything else about my situation is temporary. I keep waiting for my parents to give in and say they miss me enough to take me back however they can get me. I call them every five or six days, but it's always the same thing.

"We love you Karen, is this really what you want for yourself?"

"What do you mean?"

"Having crazy hair and living on the streets with Jack."

"I'm not living on the street! I'm staying in an apartment by the beach. I want my family to accept me the way I am. Then I can finish school and I can get a job and move out the right way. Lots of parents can handle their children not looking like them," I say.

When the inevitable argument erupts, I hang up the phone. They don't know where I am, they can't call me back, and I hope this leaves them hurt and frustrated. Jack is always there to comfort me and then criticize me and ask why I bother to call them at all. Today when I call my mom it's a little bit different.

"Have you ever heard of a group called Parents of Punkers?" My mom asks.

133

"Isn't that some anti-punk rock group?"

"No, the founder, Serena, is a lady who used to counsel violent gang members. Now she counsels punks and their parents, trying to bridge the gap between the two. Perhaps she could help us come to an understanding. Can you meet us at our house at noon tomorrow? I promise we'll drop you off wherever you want when it's over," my mom says.

"Can Jack come?"

"Karen, I really think it's best if it's only me, you and Dad, and Serena of course. But you have my word that when the meeting is over I will to take you right back to Jack tomorrow. Do we have a deal?"

"I'll be at your house tomorrow at noon." I hang up and start to cry. I know I'm hurting my mom. She's worried. She thinks Jack is a bad guy, and she doesn't think I'm safe here. I'm sad that my parents don't like me because of my hair and my clothes. What kind of understanding can we come to with this Serena person? Maybe she can help me make a deal with my mom and dad. As long as I do well in school, can't I be with Jack and look the way I want? It was never my plan to drop out of school at 14 years old. I want to grow up and be somebody.

"You have no business going to a Parents of Punkers meeting. They should change the name to Parents of New Wavers. Maybe I'll come and show them what a punk really looks like," Jack teases.

That night Jack falls asleep like he always does, happy and carefree. I lay on the couch staring at the ceiling, then get up and write in my journal by the light of my cigarette on the balcony. When morning comes I'm exhausted. I'm afraid, like I'm making a terrible mistake.

I walk alone to my parents house wearing my purple Converse high tops, the bane of my parents existence. They match my newly dyed purple bangs. Certainly when they see my purple hair, they will no longer hate the shoes. I knock on the door, but I don't try to open it.

When my mom opens the door, her grimace about my hair only lasts a moment before she asks, "Do you want to come in and have something to eat? You're early."

"No thanks. I'll wait outside." My stomach growls and I want to smoke, but I've never smoked in front of my parents before.

Getting in their car for a 30 minute drive with them to meet Serena is my giant leap of faith. I have to have faith that something is going to get better.

Serena Dank looks as if her whole life has been unfortunate. Every hardship wears on her face like a badge of sadness. It's because of her appearance that I figure she has more life experience and a greater capacity to understand me than the shrinks I've been sent to in the past. It's the most un-cool thing I can do, meeting with the founder of

"Parents of Punkers", but I want to try to find a way to work things out with my parents. Once in Serena's office, my parents accuse me of dropping out of school.

"No, I was kicked out."

"Well, you certainly aren't planning on going back with your hair like that," my mom says.

"Enroll me in public school and I will dye my hair brown."

"You can't go to South High with your brother. You will disrupt the positive atmosphere he has worked hard to create," she says.

"Enroll me at Redondo Union. It's closer to Deborah's anyway."

"Deborah is not your parent," my dad says.

"She is trying to help me stay in school."

"At Redondo High you will be in school with Jack and he will be too much of a distraction." My mom doubts my ability.

"There are a million people at Redondo High. My success is up to me!" I scream. Great, I'm fucking crying again. I promised myself I was going to stay in control.

"Can I talk to Karen alone for a few minutes?" Serena stops the scene from escalating further. My parents, chastised, go out to the tiny waiting room. I choke back my tears as best I can and gather up my strength to defend myself against this woman. I know this is the part where she will either tell me off or to try to be my new best friend.

This room doesn't have photos of tranquil mountains with trite inspirational sayings printed along the bottom like I've seen in other shrink's rooms. The two framed pieces of art on the walls are black and white abstract line drawings, and not that ink blot shit where you are tricked into interpreting; my answers always wrong. There is one bookshelf, with a couple of plants on top and two big black recliners.

Serena's face looks like God's hand accidentally smudged the drawing of her from forehead to chin, smearing, pulling all her features down, ghostlike. Her round gray eyes are framed by thick, straight, frosted hair that almost blocks her vision. Her bangs remind me of my friend's sheepdog when they would bring it back from the groomer and all its hair would be shaved except the front part above the eyes. So the dog wouldn't really know it had a haircut, so it's eyes would be protected, so the dog felt it could hide.

"I want you to trust me so I can work as a liaison between you and your parents. Do you know what that means? I want to help you and your parents communicate. I want you to all get what you want," Serena explains.

"That sounds good." I don't have any reason to trust her, but I want to.

"What you want is for them to allow you some freedom of expression," Serena says. "And what they want is for you to come back home and go to school."

"I want to go to school. I want them to quit trying to break me and Jack up. We are in love, what's wrong with that?"

"Okay, let's work on that. Will you come back with them tomorrow? I have a group that gathers here, kids and parents all meet together. It might help your parents to see that you're not the only one with different hair. It might help you to see that you can be part of the scene and still have a relationship with your parents."

Serena acts like she cares. I want her to, so I'm willing to give it a try. As long as my parents are gonna drop me back off wherever I ask, I have nothing to lose.

"Can we at least drop you off where you're staying, so we know it's a safe place? If there is an emergency, we'll know where to find you." I am not accustomed to my mom asking things, instead of telling.

I instruct them to drive to the beach, eventually telling them "I'm staying in this building right here."

I figure it's okay to show them the building because they would never be able to find the actual apartment anyway.

"Only Karen would run away from home and end up a mile *closer* to the beach." There is sarcasm in his voice, or is it jealousy?

"Will you call us tomorrow so we can plan when and where to pick you up for the meeting?" My mom looks sad. It's rare that I can read an emotion on her face; she usually has her guard up. "We love you, Karen," she says as I close the car door.

A part of me wishes I was riding back home with them, back to my two-story house on the hill with the floor plan that my family designed together. Back to my big bedroom with sliding glass doors leading out to the open deck and perfect sod grass. But those things are only the framework, the skeleton for dead flesh that won't heal. My bedroom doesn't even have a door thanks to that sledgehammer. I don't miss my actual parents. I miss the promise of what life should be that none of us can ever keep.

Back at Deborah's house, Jack opens the door. "Deborah is out for the night baby! Let's fuck in every room!" I hold him tight, needing comfort, not sex.

"I didn't think they'd bring you back. I figured I'd have to come rescue you from your parent's house tonight," he says gallantly.

It's nice to know he would come to save me, the punk rock Rapunzel. Being with Jack alone in the house, I can imagine being on my own someday. A home filled with love. We spend hours making love and after, while he is in the shower, I call my mom and tell her it was nice to see them.

"I liked Serena, maybe she can help us work something out."

"Will you come by early tomorrow, before the group with Serena, so we can talk?" My mom asks.

"About what?"

"About what you would like to happen now," my mom says, not actually saying anything, as usual.

"Well, I would like Deborah to have custody of me so I can go to school."

"Come over early tomorrow and we will talk about that then."

"I'll see if Jack and Deborah can make it."

"I don't see any reason for Jack to come," my mom says.

"He comes with me everywhere, Mom. We love each other."

"O.K. Whatever you want. Come by tomorrow at 6:00." My mom is unusually agreeable, I think, as I hang up the phone.

"Who were you talking to?" Jack asks as he comes in the room.

"My mom."

"What does she want?" he asks suspiciously.

"We are gonna meet tomorrow at my parents' house to discuss me staying here with Deborah and going back to school."

"Maybe this Parents of Punkers thing isn't so bad."

"I liked Serena, she was nice. She said she started out counseling violent gang members, then one time she got a call from a school to talk to a punk girl they didn't understand. After that she kept counseling punks. So, it's not like she's against punks. Maybe tomorrow, with you, Deborah and me, my parents will have to listen. At least you will be there to protect me."

"Of course, baby. I wouldn't have it any other way."

26 ●WIRED

We pull up to the top of my parents' street and I point to the only two-story house on the block and say, "That's it, on the right, the brown one." I can imagine what Deborah is thinking; who runs away from the biggest house on the block?

We get out of the car and I look down at our feet: purple high-tops, engineer boots and brown leather, low-heeled slouch boots step onto the brick walkway. These bricks … I think of my dad on his hands and knees, laying each one by hand. There are planters filled with evergreens that my mom and I put in the ground. My brother and his friends carried bags of wood chips to cover the dirt on top. As we walk up to the entry, I see our front door that houses a beautiful piece of etched glass artwork made for us by a family friend. Two birds perched above some flowers, sitting so close that only their outside wings are showing, suggesting they are embraced in a hug, their little beaks facing each other. Between the flowers and the perch, etched in the glass is our last name: Pigon. I don't know any other family that has a front door with their name etched in the window. On the basis of this door alone, it seems our family should have been solid.

We brought the etched glass from our old house. In that house there were two entry doors, with two identical pieces of art; four birds symbolizing each member of our family. Somewhere between that life and this, my brother began fighting in school; they said he was having emotional control issues. Mike became prone to outbursts; one act of violence resulted in a broken window. They seem to forgive his outbursts sooner and more completely than they do me. I would never smash one of those windows.

Past the beautiful etchings, through the glass, you can see the grand entrance and a staircase with a banister made out of sanded two-by-fours. My dad can't bear to install a prefabricated banister in the home he built, but has yet to get around to making the banister he has in his mind. I try to open the door, but it's locked, so I ring the doorbell. I haven't slept here in four weeks, but it hurts to know I am locked out. I watch my parents emerge from opposite ends of the house to answer the door. Deborah is warm and friendly when I introduce her to my parents, but they are barely cordial to her. They ask us to join them in the living room upstairs.

We pass photos on the wall going up the stairs. First, there is a photo of my brother standing next to a person in a giant koala suit taken at the San Diego Zoo during one of the only two family vacations we've ever taken. At the time, my brother wanted teddy bears to be his "thing". He was about 14 years old, the age I am now. Next is a professional double exposure photo of my dad, a close up of his face and a body shot of him in his karate uniform with his yellow belt, taken recently at the karate studio he built for Chuck Norris. Beside it is a similar photo of my brother in his karate *gi*, doing a high kick with his fists up, blocking his face. They look strong and handsome. I think for the most part, my brother wished that my dad wasn't in karate with him, while I secretly wished I could've gone, but it's not for girls.

The next picture on the wall is of me. I have long, feathered hair and a blue T-shirt with a parrot my mom embroidered on it back before she retired from being a mom. The photo was taken at the grand opening of the karate studio my dad built. I had a crush on Chuck Norris ever since my dad took us to see the movie *Good Guys Wear Black*, so I wanted my photo taken with him, but was too shy and embarrassed to ask. My dad told him about my crush and dragged me over to him. Then Chuck put me in a gentle headlock, while my dad took the picture. I'm smiling from ear to ear in the photo and so is Chuck, but my brother hates this picture, because I didn't walk up and get my photo standing next to him like a "normal" person.

When we get to the top of the stairs, I can tell Deborah is impressed by the high ceilings and big windows spanning two walls, the view of Redondo Beach and the Palos Verdes lights. My mom's sitting room has an opulent golden hue intentionally created by decorating with accents of brass and glass, gold toned loveseats, and a dark chocolate oversized recliner. There's no T.V. in this room, just lamps with bright bulbs for reading, and dim lights for relaxing. This room is for the adults to get away from kids, to sit, drink wine and enjoy the view.

Jack and I sit on a love seat and Deborah sits in the recliner. My parents stare from across the room, like they are sizing us up for a fight. Jack isn't trying to impress and placate my parents like he did the first time they met. This time he places his hand high up on my thigh, turning their stares into scowls. We have matching hair now, mine platinum with purple bangs, his all purple and spiked straight up with Jell-O. I take a deep breath and survey the teams; three on our side and two on theirs.

In my heart I know we are still outnumbered.

I start my pitch; "Deborah is a responsible adult. She lives in the Redondo school district, so if you sign papers, she can register me for school."

My mom looks Deborah in the eyes and asks in her cool, monotone, businesslike voice, "Do you really think that I'm going to sign away my daughter to a 26-year-old stranger?"

"I really wasn't sure. She's been at my house for a couple of weeks and things have been going well. She's a great kid and I think it's wonderful that she wants to go to school," Deborah replies.

"You think it hasn't been a problem for me that you have made it easy for my daughter to stay away from home? What makes you qualified to take over the parenting of my daughter? Are you prepared to handle all of the responsibilities, or only the jobs you think are fun?" My mom continues her rapid fire and it's obvious that Deborah isn't equipped to handle her. No one ever is. It's only a matter of minutes before my mom has Deborah stumbling over her own words and doubting her ability to handle me full-time. Even Jack is speechless. He sits there with his mouth slightly open, but his body is at full attention, tense and on guard.

I want to save Deborah from my mom, but I don't know how. There's nothing I could've said to Deborah to prepare her for my mom. In the weeks I've been gone, I've felt my confidence increase. My soul has grown ten feet. In the last fifteen minutes, I have shrunk into a helpless child who doesn't even have command of basic language yet. They will never compromise with me. I'm ready to go. I need to get out of this house.

My dad leans over and whispers like we are in some sort of conspiracy together,

"I wrote you a poem."

"You did?" I can only recall him ever writing one poem before; it's framed and on the wall next to my mom's side of the bed. "Can I read it?"

"Sure." He takes a dramatic pause.

"Let me see it," I ask.

"Why don't you come to the room, where you can give it your full attention? It seems like mom and Deb are going to talk for a few more minutes."

"Okay."

Getting up off the loveseat, I try to apologize with my eyes as I look at Deborah.

"I'll be right back, and then we can go," I say to Deborah and Jack.

My parents bedroom takes up the rest of the second level of the house. There's the master bedroom area, marble-topped night stands flanking the king-sized bed and lamps that pull out accordion-style so you can read in bed if you want.

On the south side of my parents bedroom is a little room that was supposed to become a library. There's a big window with the same spectacular view of Palos Verdes, and French doors opening to a balcony overlooking our backyard. The ceiling in this room is 16 feet high with deep stained open beams and two big skylights. There's an alcove notched out of the top 6 feet of wall. My dad wanted to put in an aviary for finches. He likes the way they sound and thought it would be a peaceful effect to read in the sunny library and listen to the finches chirp. My mom said absolutely not. She's the one that would have to climb a ladder to clean the filthy birdcage. Plus, why have birds in cages that you can't even see? That little alcove is an empty space, a shrine to disagreements, unfinished projects, our vacant family.

On the north side of their bedroom are two more French doors that open to a walk-in closet. My dad walks through these doors, stopping at my mom's long dressing table with the movie star lights and make up mirror. He hands me a stack of pale blue paper with a handwritten poem.

●■●■●■●■●■●■●■●■●■●■●■●■●

My greatest wish—
To be a dad.
And praised be God,
A child was had.
The love grew strong, my wife, a mother.
And thanks to God, we had another.
Our love is full, our bond is strong,
The four of us, we sing our song.
Our melody of life is dear,
We sing it loud, for all to hear.
Rhythm, tempo, is at our pace.
What joy, to share this human race.
With lows and highs,
Some flats, some sharps.
I even hear angelic harps.
First movement done, and two to go.
Our song becomes a picture show.
The tempo quickens, with flashing scenes.
Our children now —are in their teens.
They're adding their notes to our melody.
Can we keep up? Is there still harmony?
The tempo's even quicker now.
It came from where? I can't see how:
Another tune? A different sound?
They're not the ones that I have found.
STOP THE MUSIC,
STOP THE BAND.
I CAN NOT FIND
MY DAUGHTER'S HAND:
And now there's "punk"—

The slam and speed.
Won't someone help us
Fill our need?
I still have two more movements to go.
MY song's not finished, please let it flow.

●■●■●■●■●■●■●■●■●■●■●■●■●

Tears. I can't help it, I don't like causing pain. I'm not trying to be a bad person, I know I am a disappointment. But I've spent the last 14 years feeling like I've outstayed my welcome. I want out. I can't survive this family.

"I like your poem Dad. Don't worry about me. I'm going to be okay, I promise to stay in school if you guys will enroll me at Redondo High. Can I keep your poem? I'd really like to have it."

"Sure."

"Thanks." I give my dad a half-hug, and step towards the door.

He stands between the doors and me. "You're going to stay here," my dad says, "I meant everything in that poem. But it's time for you to come home, and you're staying home tonight." He has this authoritative voice, empowered by being in charge, leaning against the doors so I am trapped in.

Before I can devise a plan, I hear a knock on the closet doors, my mom's voice saying, "It's me, let me in."

"You used your poem to trick me?" I ask, betrayed.

Oh my God, the two of them planned this whole thing all along. They were never even considering letting me live with Deborah and going to school. They were too lazy to even come and get me. They tricked me into walking right into their house. They pretended to care about what I wanted. They pretended to act like I mattered.

"They're gone," my mom tells my dad as he lets her in.

"What?" I ask. Yeah, I know the answer, but I need to hear it. I didn't hear any screaming, I didn't hear Jack yelling for me, or vowing to come back and rescue me.

"Deborah and Jack are gone." My mom is so matter-of-fact.

"How did you make them leave?"

"I told Deborah that you are my daughter and I am keeping you here; if they didn't leave immediately I would call the police. If she ever tries to move you into her house again, I will press charges."

"How could you do this to me? How could you trap me? I trusted you!"

No one fought for me? There were no raised voices, no sounds of a struggle. No fought for me? No one yelled, "*We're sorry we have to leave you here!*" as they got pushed out. How could Jack and Deborah

144

leave without a word? I can't believe I've been kidnapped back home.

"I HATE YOU!" I yell and then howl and scream like they are ripping my limbs from my body. Surrounded by my parents' clothes in their walk-in closet, I know no one outside these walls can hear me. They could cut me up with my dad's rotary saw right now and no one would hear.

"If you continue to scream, I will call the police and they will take you to Harbor General Hospital and keep you for 24 hours in their mental health unit." She says like she has called ahead and verified these details. I believe her, and collapse into a pile of tears and defeat. There are many closed doors between me and freedom now; no reason to fight.

I had it all worked out. I had food, shelter, freedom, someone to love me. I could go to gigs, look the way I want to look. All I needed was to go to school, so I could grow up and be somebody. My parents killed it all. They stand above me victorious.

"I'm sure it will be hard for you to sleep, since you're used to sleeping in someone's arms every night," my mom says with bitterness.

Why does she hate that someone wants to hold me?

Then her voice changes; it's even, rehearsed, like she's reading from a script. "Let's go downstairs and get some pajamas from your room." She is making an effort to sound like she cares. The three of us walk down the stairs together, my dad in front, my mom in back. Sandwiched by my jailers.

My bedroom looks different. It takes a moment to notice all the little things that they've removed, pictures I've had up, albums, cassette tapes, stickers. Anything that *they* didn't care for was removed while I was gone. I'm sure they went through every inch of my room. The things they left behind no longer represent me; a volleyball poster, my 4-foot-tall stuffed giraffe. They are trying to erase the last year of my life and plop me into a T.V. set so I can be re-cast as the preppy teenager they wish I was.

I'm standing with pajamas in hand, unsure of what to do next.

"Put your pajamas on in the bathroom," my mom explains. "Don't lock the door or stay in there too long. Dad will be outside the bathroom window, you can't climb out."

I was about to say "thanks" but thought better of it. I closed the door and worked on a plan. I could jump out the tiny bathroom window and crash as hard as I can onto my dad and then run away. At 5'2", 98 pounds, it is more likely we would end up an injured pile, ruining my only chance of escape. If I did run away again, then what? Where would I go? I can't go to Deborah's house, they would send the police straight there. Can't go to Jack's; that would be the second place they'd look.

The list of places I can't go is long.

The list of places I can go is long. I can go anywhere, it's a great big world out there, but I don't want to be alone in it.

I will bide my time and make a plan; in the meantime, take advantage of all the "comforts of home". The toothpaste, fresh and minty, the towel fluffy and soft. I haven't had a towel that wasn't damp and smelling like must and mold since the night I ran away. I need to set myself up to leave again, get some money and supplies.

Walking out of the bathroom in fresh pajamas, I follow my mom to the downstairs living room where the hide-a-bed has already been pulled out. My mom sits down with her legs out in front of her and I sit beside her, cross-legged. Sitting this close is awkward and unnatural for us.

"I'm going to wire your ankle to Mom's so you can't sneak out tonight," my dad says, pulling a spool of wire out from under the bed.

"Oh my God!" He can't possibly mean it. My dad doesn't even make our dogs wear a collar. He's being dramatic again, like crumbling his carton of cigarettes.

"You aren't really going to tie me up to Mom, right?"

"Believe me, I don't want to be tied up like a prisoner here either, but I'm not going to have you running around in the streets," my mom says.

It's like they got their stolen car back, so now they are putting extra locks on the garage.

"I promise I won't leave. I will be here in the morning to talk. Please, please don't tie us, don't wire us."

He ignores me, talking through his process out loud, like he does when he doesn't want anyone to contribute their thoughts to a project he's unsure of.

"I'll wrap it around here a few times, not tight enough to cut off circulation, but not so loose that you can slip out. Then I will make a few twists in the middle so that there is some distance between your foot and mom's." I can see my mom getting irritated with him; he continues so she can't interject. I can't believe I'm literally tied in the middle of this; wired, in fact.

A pack of cigarettes are on the table next to the couch; I reach over and grab one and light it up. How can a man who's tying me to another person with wire deny me a cigarette? My mom looks surprised for a moment, then hands me the ashtray from the table beside her, a small act of acquiescence.

Smoking in bed, watching my dad twist wire around my ankle; this scene is what you would call ironic. A few days ago, after amazing sex, I was in this same position; smoking in bed watching Jack untie my feet. I wonder if I told this to my dad, would he stop, or make the restraints tighter?

"Tomorrow, I'll fix the locks on your room so you can sleep in there." I don't know what he means but I want him to shut up and finish his perverted project. I want to fall into sleep so this nightmare will end.

27 ● HOME EC. IN THE WILD WEST

Mom is awake and sitting up when I open my eyes. There's still wire around my ankle but she and I are no longer attached—the connection has been cut. What do I feel? Panic? Betrayal? I only want to get up and take a shower. I feel dirty.

"Good morning," my mom says. It's an odd greeting to receive from your captor as they lie next to you in bed.

"Good morning, Mom. Now what?" I mean that in terms of the conversation as well as the rest of my life. My parents are always lecturing me about how I am such a follower of Jack and the punk scene and why can't I be an 'individual'. Yet it seems their biggest goal is for me to follow them blindly into every decision of my life.

"We are going to register you to attend West High" my Mom says.

"You have not earned the right to leave the house," my dad says as he joins us in the living room. "Until you restore our faith in you, you are on 'probation'. At night we will lock you in your room, because we can't trust you not to roam the streets like a stray dog."

"So basically you are calling me a bitch?" I want to fight with them. I don't want them to be so calm as they spell out my life, like they have this all planned out and for once they are a united front, joining forces against me.

"No one is calling you a bitch." Mom, the great negotiator, steps in. "What we want to make clear is that you are home now and you will be staying here."

My dad has screwed the sliding door and windows closed so they won't open at all. The door knob has been turned around so that it locks from the outside. "Every night you will be locked inside; we will unlock the door in the morning." This seems about right, but then they say

149

something very surprising.

"You will be allowed to see Jack every other weekend under our supervision, and you may talk to him twice a week on the phone. Of course we will be listening in. Serena feels the more we try to keep you from him, the more you will want to be together. Our hope is that as you broaden your circle of friends outside of the punk scene and you gain some distance from Jack, you will realize that you're too smart and too good for him."

I can't recall my mom ever saying I was good at anything. I would be flattered or proud if she wasn't trying to manipulate me, to keep me away from the only person who truly loves and accepts me.

Then they lock me in my room, so they can get ready for their day. I hear my dad's footsteps upstairs and the smells of my mom cooking breakfast. I go into my walk-in closet and slide the door closed. My parents didn't find all the things I had taped to the inside of this door. The lyrics to the Germs song "Manimal" are still taped inside. So are Tammy's funny stick man drawings: the drunken stick man with the wobbly legs, the stick man with a giant penis, the stick man hanging from a noose. The tiny little details she adds make the drawings so funny.

I slide open the closet door and search for something to wear. Clothes that used to be okay for me to wear are missing: plain Levi's 501 jeans, my ET surfboards T-shirt, my vintage shirt-waist dresses. What are left are clothes I haven't worn in over a year, champagne-colored corduroy pants, striped boat necked shirt.

Mom knocks, why? She knows I am locked in here.

"Yes," I say to the door.

"Breakfast is ready," my mom says, as she unlocks the door. She surveys me and says, "You look nice." I don't even want to bother discussing how these clothes make me feel; she wouldn't understand or care.

After breakfast, the first stop is West High admissions office. The idea of a fresh start at West is appealing, but the fantasy crumbles as I am met with funny looks by the administration. Right away they let us know I can't attend school there with purple hair. My mom assures them the purple will be gone by tonight. The remaining registration takes only moments. Mom hands over the papers she has already filled out, then they hand me a map and a schedule. Except to prove I actually exist, there was no reason for me to be there.

Then it's off to Norwalk to see Serena, who swears she has nothing to do with my parents kidnapping me. But I feel betrayed when she says "They must really care to go to such great lengths to have you back."

"If they really cared, wouldn't they love me no matter what color my hair is?"

"I think purple hair is too foreign to them. You're going to have to give up on that demand for now," she tells me.

"They took away all my clothes! I don't even have any Levi's that I can wear to my first day of school tomorrow. I'm wearing pants I haven't worn in over a year!"

"Is there anything wrong with Levi's jeans?" Serena asks my parents.

"Well, that depends on how she wears them I suppose," my mom answers. "She could make them look punk or normal."

"But PUNK is NORMAL," I yell.

"Karen, I'm trying to help you negotiate," Serena says.

"Okay, what if I wear the shirt I have on now, but with Levi's instead of these cords?"

"That will be acceptable," my mom says.

Everyone is exhausted and no one is truly happy. At least in the end of the "negotiations" I get to keep my hair blonde and not dye it back brown, but I have to remove the purple from my bangs.

* * * * * * * * * * * * *

Day two as their prisoner, my mom drops me off at school for my first day at West. I'm instructed to be in the exact same spot when school lets out. Walking to my first class I fantasize about leaving out the back gate. It would be really easy to do, but just as easy for my parents to come find me again. I will try to make this work; the option to run is always there.

West High is filled with stoner kids who listen to Led Zeppelin. Redondo High has more surfers and South High, where my brother attends, is filled with rich preppy jocks.

"Are you new?" the kid at the desk next to me asks before class starts. He looks like the kind of person who would normally beat up a punk; preppy hair parted on the side, football jersey in the school colors, last name across the back.

"Do you know Bill? They call him Bill Jacket?" The jock asks.

"Nah, I don't know anyone, it's my very first class here."

"Oh, he's a punk, like you."

"I didn't know there were any punks at this school." I feel happy to know this guy can tell I'm a punk, despite the clothes my parents have left for me to choose from. I guess it's my ultra-short hair that's tipping him off. Even though it's a sort of natural-looking blonde color, my mom says it's so short I look like a "chemo patient" with bangs.

"There's only one punk here. Well, now there are two."

"Do you guys kick his ass all the time?" I wonder what their tolerance is.

"Nah, Bill is hilarious. He wears crazy clothes. You look pretty normal compared to him." His words are like a knife in my heart. Now once this Bill character sees me, he's gonna think I'm a poseur.

Second period class is Home Economics and the teacher looks at me like I have just landed from Mars. She appears to have been unpacked from a time capsule sealed in 1951. Her lesson today is how to cut up a whole chicken, something I have absolutely no interest in doing. I only eat animals smaller than me, and not often. I certainly don't handle them raw with my bare hands.

"I would like to be excused from this lesson because I am a vegetarian."

"You don't have to kill or eat the chicken, but in order to get credit, you have to prepare and participate with your group." Her tone is condescending, like she has this conversation every time butchering chickens comes up in class, and she's almost tired of winning the debate.

"It's my first day, I don't have a group."

She sends me to a table with four other students. One of the girls is cute and tiny, her straight leg jeans rolled up with wide cuffs at the bottom. Her hair isn't feathered as much as curled tightly with a curling iron on each side, so her face looks like it's framed with shiny blonde sausages. She's wearing a baseball shirt with a Lynyrd Skynyrd concert logo. I could never fit in with her circle of friends, but she smiles at me.

"Could you hand me the knife?" I ask.

"You can kick back, I cook chickens all the time at my house. It's easy."

"Nah, let me do this for the teacher. Is there a knife sharpener around?" I ask.

Blonde sausage girl points to an electric knife sharpener on the counter.

"This is going to be easier with a super sharp knife," I say to no one in particular as I walk over and press my knife into the sharpener. The loud grinding noise causes the teacher and most of the class to look towards me.

In one swift motion I pull the knife off the sharpener, push my sleeve up on my arm, and make a big slice across. "I would rather cut myself than cut up this chicken," I proclaim, as I watch the teacher's face turn white, and then a faint shade of green.

Silence.

Mrs. Home Ec. Teacher stands there with her slightly bouffant hair that probably hasn't changed in 25 years. Her frosted white, almond-shaped nails reach to cover her wide open mouth.

I hear a few whispers in the background, "What happened?"

"That new girl cut herself."

"She got cut?"

"No, she cut herself!"

"Go to the office!" The teacher commands.

"The office?" I stare her down, still holding the knife in my hand. I can't feel blood oozing from the cut on my arm; I wish I had cut deeper so this whole scene would look more dramatic.

"The nurse's office," she concedes. "Please go to the nurse's office and have your arm bandaged. You can spend the rest of the period lying down in there."

I drop the knife in the sink, grab a paper towel, and leave.

I'm not hurt and don't want to be in trouble. Wrapping the paper towel around my arm and pulling my sleeve over it, I feel empowered, like I am wearing Wonder Woman's gold cuff. I've cut the first day of school anxiety right out of me and I'm ready to walk into another room full of strangers, their eyes all on me, judging me.

My plan is to hide in the bathroom til next period, walk into next class like nothing happened. Lucky for me, I land in the bathroom where a half dozen "bad girls" are smoking.

"Do you know Bill Jacket?" one of them asks as she hands me a Lucky Strike cigarette.

"No, but I hear he's the only punk at this school."

"He's not the only one," she says, as we look each other over. This girl is beautiful and talks with a bit of a British accent. Her name is Melanie and she has short-ish, straight black hair and creamy, pale skin. I feel stupid as I talk to her because most of what I say is a lie.

"Oh thank you, I normally smoke unfiltered cigarettes. Yes, my family spends summers in England, because my family is British."

The more pronounced her accent is, the more I develop one. This is me as a new person, at a new school. For absolutely no reason at all, I am desperate for this girl to like me, but how can I can keep this up? What the fuck is wrong with me?

"If you want to meet at lunch, I'll show you were we can sneak off and smoke without getting caught." I agree, promising myself that when we meet again, I won't talk with an accent.

In my next class it's more of the same: "Are you new? Do you know Bill Jacket?"

At lunch, I meet up with Melanie. We walk off campus and go around the corner to sit and have a cigarette. Nervous, I still talk like an idiot with an accent and now it seems too late to stop. Melanie graciously doesn't call me out on it. I can't gauge my emotions about girls anymore. I'm happy that anyone wants to talk or pay me any attention. I'm eager, smitten, overjoyed to have a new friend. I'm impressed by Melanie, but she looks "normal" enough for my mom to tolerate, maybe. I'm excited about the possibility of a friendship with someone that my parents won't hate or forbid me from seeing. I have butterflies in my stomach, but can't tell if that is because I am in lust with Melanie or nervous because we're not supposed to be off campus. It's likely my parents are circling the school to look for me.

After lunch it seems that the rest of my teachers have already heard the story about what happened in Home Ec. and they're afraid of me. I am invited to sit towards the back of the class and relax. Seems that if I shut up and leave the teachers alone, I won't have to do any work, which is fine with me.

The last period of the day is typing. I sit in the back of the class relieved that the day is almost over. A tall, thin kid with spiked black hair and a leather jacket with about 10 extra pounds of pins and spikes on it walks in. Bill Jacket. Only one open seat is left in the class, next to me. We finally meet, sitting side by side.

"You must be Bill Jacket."

"Yeah, Bill. You're the girl that cut herself in Home Ec."

"Yeah," I say real casually, like I do that kind of shit all the time.

"I'm K.P. Why are you in typing? It's usually only for girls."

"Because it's easy," Bill says. "What about you? Do you plan to become a secretary?"

"It's the only class they could fit me in. I need the credits."

By the end of class we conclude we don't have many friends in common, but we do like a lot of the same bands. It's inevitable our meeting was anticlimactic, having been built up all day.

At the end of the day, my mom is parked directly in front of the school exit. She must have gotten here an hour early to secure this spot.

"How was your first day of school?" my mom says cheerfully.

"Fine, I guess." It seems mom hasn't gotten a call from the Home Economics teacher yet. If you have to start a new school mid-semester, cutting yourself might be the answer if you want to be left alone.

28 ● MADE FOR T.V.

Two weeks later we are back at Serena's office; adults on folding metal chairs pushed around the perimeter of the room, kids sitting on the floor.

"We agreed on a midnight curfew, but they come wandering home whenever they feel like it." A complaint other parents have in common.

"I got home as soon as we could get back from the gig." A sixteen year old boy explains.

"The kids here are my age or slightly older, ran away, and now have more freedom than I have ever had." I say towards my Mom. "Aren't you just happy to have your kids back home safe and in school?" I ask the other parents.

"We are so grateful to have our children home with us, we know their appearance and musical taste is of no importance, so long as we are all together as a family." And then my family embraced me and brought me home and bought me engineer boots. In my mind, that was how this moment should unfold, but in reality, my mom asked the other kids;

"Are any of you engaging in this self-mutilation?"

Punks and parents look towards me. They turn against me.

"What the hell do you do that for?"

"That kind of shit makes you look stupid!" says the boy who told us ten minutes ago he has beat up kids and left them for dead.

"Yeah, it makes us all look stupid," says a person who hasn't said a single thing during the whole meeting. They are empowered in a group attack. Nothing brings people closer together than the mutual hatred of another.

A pretty girl wearing pumps and narrow pants that accentuate her spidery legs tells me, "You beat yourself up because you're too weak to beat up anyone else."

"That's not true," I barely whisper in defense.

But it's true. There are plenty of people I'd beat up if I thought it would change anything, but I know I can't make others feel my pain.

"When I cut myself, something is different," I try to explain; "I've taken the hurt out of my heart and mind and put it on the outside, on my skin."

"That has nothing to do with Punk Rock, that's emotional manipulation," another boy says.

Mom wins again.

Leaving the meeting completely defeated, Serena takes us aside and asks if we would be willing to be on a T.V. talk show with her. I'm shocked when my mom agrees. Several of the kids have done interviews before, some of them even got to go to New York to be on the Phil Donahue show. Perhaps this is my initiation into their pack.

"You're the only kid who cuts themselves," Mom says, breaking the uncomfortable silence on our car ride home. As if that makes me worse than the other kids.

"I am the only kid whose parents lock them in their room and control what they wear." I think my parents are worse than the others.

"Our participation in this television show is not for you to recruit more punks. It's to help Serena reach out to more families."

"I know, Mom." She turned the kids against me, like she turned Gina and her family against me.

My few phone calls with Jack are forced and hollow, I don't want to ask him where he's been or what he's been doing when my parents listen in. I can't imagine any of us would like his answer.

Our secret moments together before school are sabotaged by my insecurities. I promise myself not to nag him, but words escape my lips.

"What have you been doing, or should I ask, WHO have you been doing while my parents hold me hostage?" I try to be light and sassy. Jack is not fooled.

"Come on K.P., don't be like that. We only have a little time together, unless you want to ditch school and come home with me."

"I can't ditch, Jack, can't we just talk a minute?" He has no idea of the punishment getting caught would bring upon me.

"If we only have a minute, why waste it talking." He leans in for a kiss.

After a few minutes of making out, his hands start creeping under my shirt. I want him to stop, but don't say it. I felt loved and connected when we were together twenty-four hours a day, now I'm getting groped under my top before I go to class. *We don't have time, but we have passion, this is what passion feels like,* I tell myself. When the bell rings he walks me to class, then leaves to whatever and whoever he fancies, while I walk the halls of hippies.

On the day of the television interview, my mom picks me up from school.

"You need to change clothes."

"What are you talking about? We are supposed to be ourselves on the show, not what you want me to be."

"You are our daughter, not a punk. If you want to be interviewed, change clothes. You will not do it looking like a punk."

For forty miles I look down at the horrible light blue corduroy pants and stupid white moccasins that cover half my body and all of my self confidence. We arrive at a big convention hall, not a fancy movie studio like I imagined. The interviewer is wearing a blue high-collared power suit with white piping. It looks like a uniform, militant. Her blonde feathered hair is pulled back on one side, just like I wore in 6th grade.

Serena's done several interviews before; she is good at this. She says she is not against punk rock, she wants to reunite parents with their children. She worries about young kids internalizing the message of the music and the violence in the scene.

The interviewer asks about the cigarette burns and cuts on my arms. My parents forbade me to discuss this on T.V., and I don't want to talk about it. I use my love of the Germs (band) as an explanation for it. I'm uncomfortable, ill-prepared, dressed up like someone I am not, on display for punks to laugh at and other parents to blame for all the pain in my family.

"Do you have any parting words, something final to say?" the interviewer asks.

"Try to understand your children," were my final words on *The Sunday Show*".

A few weeks later, we do a second interview. I am no longer locked in my room at night, although I don't know when they stopped; it was never discussed. At some point they silently tricked me to be their project, instead of their prisoner. Despite our continued discomfort with each other, we believe that Parents of Punkers will heal our family Who knows why we agreed to a second television interview, probably in an attempt to reinforce our faith

For the filming of *LA Morning*, we arrive at an actual studio, it's cool to see behind the scenes of T.V. Not until we are ushered into a small room do I notice my parents and Serena speaking in hushed tones. I am the only one in the room they are withholding information from.

"What's happening? What's going on?"

Silence falls, and it takes an abnormal amount of time before only Serena answers my direct question. "Lee Ving, the singer for the band FEAR, is going to join us for the interview. We didn't agree to this."

Trying to play down my excitement, I mutter an offhand "Oh," turning my head to hide my smile. I'm a fan of the band FEAR, and now I have someone here on my side!

The interview lady comes into the cramped room asking if I can tell her anything about the band. My parents are quick to tell her all that they know. She was surprised to learn that my dad had seen FEAR perform. He tells her about the awful, disgusting lyrics.

"Can you sing me a little bit of a song?" Interview Lady asks.

"This isn't the type of music you *sing*, and they aren't going to let me say the lyrics out loud," I tell her.

"Do you think you could write any of it down? It would probably be better if I had it in writing anyway."

"Fine," my mom says. "Then when we recite some of the lyrics on television, people will have a better idea what we're dealing with."

On a yellow legal pad I write out the lyrics to "I love Livin' in the City."

♬ My house smells just like the zoo,
It's chock full of shit and puke!
Cockroaches on the walls
Crabs crawlin' on my balls!
Ohh, but I'm so clean cut,
I just wanna fuck some slut! ♬

By the time, I have written the word "puke" their comments begin.

"There's no way you're going to get him to admit to writing *that*," my mom says.

"There is no way I'm allowed to say *that* on television," the interviewer says after I write the word "balls."

My dad says "I can't believe this is the stuff trapped in my daughter's head, taking up space in her mind."

They're overreacting, it's a fucking song! It can't reach out and hit you. The song can't smash your door in with a sledgehammer. I continue writing the lyrics because I hate everyone around me.

♬ Spent my whole life in the city,
Where junk is king and the air smells shitty.

People pukin' everywhere.
Piles of blood, scabs and hair.
Bodies wasted in defeat,
People dyin' on the street,
But the suburban scumbags, they don't care,
They just get fat and dye their hair! ♫

Interview Lady takes the legal pad, leads us to a fake living room with bright lights and cameras. I sit down next to my parents and across from Lee Ving, then time stops. I notice he is old, closer to my parent's age than mine. How did he become a punk singer and my parents became yuppies? How did I end up here, across from the guy who performed at the first gig I went to? Then, just like that, time went fast-forward, and then caught up, and I am looking down at a monitor and listening to my mom say, "She was gone for four weeks. I saw burns on her arms and tattoos on her legs. The punk rock thing started last summer ...."

I don't know how to defend myself, how to say that my parents blame the scene for everything wrong with our family. I know it's the scene that has saved me from everything wrong with our family.

The interviewer asks Lee, "What about the dress? What are you trying to say when you dress that way?"

"I'm trying to say I care about the way I dress, if I didn't I would look like them," Lee says towards us. The monitor shows this dork shaking her head, caught in the crossfire, wearing a red striped shirt and corduroy pants. I'd be less humiliated if I was actually naked right now. My mind screams, "Speak up! Stand up for yourself!" but I'm no match for this man who's given so many interviews and performs on stage every week. He is winning and I am an idiot.

During the commercial break Lee unhooks his microphone, says, "I'm not doing this anymore," and walks off the set. I'm glad he's gone, if he's not going to be on my side.

Three months after my dad wired me and my mom together, we agree to do an interview with *Hour Magazine*. "They will come to our home and interview each one of us separately, so we can all tell our own story." The promise of redemption.

The interview lady from *Hour Magazine* seems kind. We sat in the living room and started talking. After a while I forgot about the two guys behind the two cameras. It was just me and her and she didn't seem to be making me out to be a bad guy

"What is it you want out of life?" she asks in a caring tone.

"I want to graduate, get a job, and move out on my own, so I don't have people telling me what to do."

I got to speak my dreams and my truth with her, but even my parents won't hear me until the show plays on T.V. The lady said it would take a few months.

When the crew was finished packing up their cameras and lights, Interview Lady tells me "I hope that you and your family can find a way to get along. My son is in a hospital right now because he has a problem with drugs." As she hugs me goodbye she says, "I'm so grateful that he isn't a punk."

* * * * * * * * * * * *

I'm barely getting by at West; every night I plan to do my homework, but end up writing and quietly listening to secret punk cassettes. I try to stay out of their way; my mom calls it "isolating". My next report card will bring a new level of punishment and discipline, or worse; they threaten regularly to send me away if my "grades and attitude don't improve." On weekends my mom makes me go with her to the library to research boarding schools; it's like having to tie my own noose.

Jack often meets me before school. I can't help but wonder if he is coming from another girl's house; why else would he be up so early?

One day he shows up at lunch with blood on his shirt, his face bruised and his hand bandaged.

"What happened?"

"I got jumped last night."

"What do you mean, 'jumped'? Why?"

"They took my chains, hit me and kicked me." He starts smiling, pretends to flip long hair over his shoulder. "They hurt my feelings when they told me I looked stupid."

"Oh Jack, I'm so sorry."

"Don't worry about me, next time we're alone you can kiss all my boo-boos."

Melanie and Jack are the only two bright spots in my day. Sometimes, when my parents are at work, I skate to Melanie's house for a visit after school. Melanie writes on her mattress with pen; she says her mother doesn't mind, because sheets cover the mattress. I know this thought is unwarranted and unrealistic, but maybe since her mom doesn't mind writing on a mattress, she wouldn't mind another person sleeping on her floor? I know it's insane, but I seek out this fantasy often and use it for comfort.

One night, while chain smoking and writing poetry, I decide it would be a good idea to tell Melanie exactly how I feel.

Dear Melanie,

I'm not sure who it is I am made to love. I love everyone. Why does it matter what a person has between their legs? Why wouldn't a person be able to completely love a man OR a woman? Most of the "girl stuff" is still in my mind, I haven't had many opportunities to act on those feelings, but I'd like you to change that.

"I hope no matter what, we can still be friends after you read this." I say as I dig the note out of my backpack and hand it to Melanie at the end of the school week.

* * * * * * * * * * * * *

Over the weekend I become sick as I have ever been. No voice, a sore throat and a fever. On Monday a doctor determines I've got laryngitis and bronchitis, prescribes antibiotics and codeine cough syrup and says I can go back to school at the end of next week. I lay on the living room hide-a-bed, propped up and watching T.V. I don't have to talk to anyone, I write everything down on a pad so my voice will heal. I fall to sleep watching television.

One night, instead of making me go to bed in my own room, my mom woke me up and gave me a pill. I remember her saying it was "To help me sleep", but I was already asleep.

29 ● MAGIC WAND

JULY 13, 1982   **Aurora, Colorado**

Happy birthday to me.

I'm 15 years old.

I am an old 15 years.

Two months ago, I had all the freedom in the world, walked along the beach at night, and had adventures in Hollywood. Now I'm a prisoner in a youth center where I'm the only privately placed kid surrounded by criminals. For some reason my parents think this is better than letting me go.

An entire lifetime ago, I thought I'd be released by my birthday; now I am looking forward to my next first cigarette.

I'm called from class to the director's office; a box addressed to me in my mom's writing sits on his wide desk. I hate him. I hate the way his chin is always tilted up, looking down his nose at everyone, puffing on his stupid pipe like he's Sherlock Holmes. He's short and round and I hate that he revels in the power that he has over us. Why does he have to watch me open this box? No matter what kind of response he expects, I will not give it to him. Inside are new sweatpants to accommodate my increasing girth, cassette tapes of parent approved music—Elvis Costello, the Go-Go's, the B-52s — and a jar of those new, fancy little jellybeans with the flavor that goes all the way through. When I set the jar down, the director picks it up and helps himself to a handful.

The largest item in my birthday box is a photo album. My life story in photos.

"How do you feel when you look at those photos?" Dick Director asks. He wants to shrink me, pull out my emotions and use them against me.

"This is only part of the story; these photos only show a part of my family life. The part they wanted you to see. There aren't even any photos of me from the last year of my life, because they don't like the way I look."

"You can't appreciate the effort your mother put into this?" Director Dick asks.

"They are denying that an entire part of my life existed. Like they didn't have a daughter once I cut my hair short."

He does not debate this with me, which doesn't mean he agrees with my opinion, just that my opinion doesn't matter. He hands me the letter,

"You don't have to read this out loud, but you have to read it now," Director Dickead says.

My heart is racing, could this be what I have been wishing for during these last three months at Excelsior? Am I holding the best birthday present ever—a letter saying when I get to go home?

Dear Karen,
Sometime around the New Year's Eve Gig, Jack met and started seeing a girl named Patty. Patty went to Redondo Union High, that's where she met Jack. Patty became attached to Jack and started ditching school with him. When they ditched they would sometimes go to Tricia's house. One time one of the neighbors called the police because of the noise and kids at Tricia's. The police took Patty to Redondo Union, found out her name and then called her mom to come and get her. Patty didn't dress like a punk or look like one. She was listening to punk and seeing Jack a lot. Her grades in school dropped drastically. She had been an honor student. She told her mom she wanted to be in the special education classes with Jack so she could help him. She began to cut her arms and was often in depression. Patty went out one evening and didn't return when she was supposed to. That had begun to happen frequently. Patty's dad went looking for her at about midnight. He saw Patty walking with Jack on a street not far from where Patty lives. He got out of his car and approached them. Jack stood in a fighting stance and Patty's dad hit Jack in the nose. That's how his nose was broken. Jack fell on the sidewalk and Patty and her dad got in the car and drove around for a while talking.

Jack picked himself up and went to Patty's house intending to do harm to Patty's mom. He was screaming at the door, "Let me in, I'll kill you–You F___ B___." Patty's mom had been sleeping and knew nothing of what happened. She quickly got out of bed and ran to the phone to call the police. She didn't know who was at the door. While she was talking to the police, Jack put his hand through the glass in the door and unlocked the deadbolt from inside. That's how his knuckles were broken. Patty's mom ran out the back door and went to neighbors. Jack went in the house and searched every room for her. He was bleeding from his nose and cuts on his hand, and the blood dripped on the floor throughout the house. When the police arrived he was still in the house. Then Patty's mom returned as well as Patty and her dad. After much confession and conversation, Jack's mom was called and she came to get him. Eventually Patty was placed, at her request, at Charter Pacific Hospital. Patty wanted to get away from Jack and stop the destruction to herself. Sometime during her stay there, her attitude began to change again. She blamed herself for Jack getting kicked out of Redondo Union and told her mom all she wanted was Jack and she would go to him as soon as she was released. This was in May. Perhaps Patty's attitude changed because Jack's mom called Patty at Charter Pacific and told Patty what a good influence she was on Jack and when she got out it would be great if they could be boyfriend and girlfriend again. Jack was able to get at least one note to Patty while she was in Charter Pacific. Ironically, Patty has the reputation of being gay.

Jack has a history of violence to women and continues today. He called Serena and left a message on her tape that said he was going to kill her and her children. He has abused you and many other girls.

I am afraid of him and his mother. She lied to me many times about him. I'm afraid for your brother when he leaves his job late, after the mall is closed.

That is why we told Jack, and everyone, you were at your grandparents' home in Arkansas. Since the beginning of September, I've told people you are in boarding school. I hope you will consider our safety, Karen. Jack is still close by and could want revenge for us taking you away from him.

Perhaps you know all of this Karen. I feel it is important that you know that we know, and that you know what we told people.

One of the staff should be with you now and I hope you talk to them about your feelings as you finish this letter.

My wish was that I could have told you this in person. I could have answered any questions and watched your expressions as you read, which would have given me a clue to your feelings. I must trust that the staff is watching your expressions and if you have questions you can call or write me.

Loving you—
Mom.

Dickhead is staring at me.

"Is there anything you'd like to talk about?"

"No thanks, this has been the best birthday ever," I say sarcastically.

How could Jack have been with another girl? We were living together and inseparable for four weeks! Where was that Patty girl then? What my mom said could be true, how else would she know about Jack's broken nose? The seed of doubt has been planted. I keep reaching into my brain trying to eradicate it, but it's just out of reach. If I continue to dig deeper, I will only destroy my mind.

"When you start to appreciate what your parents have done for you, then you can have their gifts."

He's trying to make me lose my temper, but I won't.

"Thanks," I say sweetly, "Enjoy my presents until then."

Through a mouthful of jellybeans the director says, "You can head back to class."

30 ● SURRENDER

AUGUST, 1982 ▪Fifteen and one month▪   **Aurora, Colorado**

I have been living with thirty girls in a cottage named Shalom for a month now. If the color blue on the walls was a crayon it would say "Mental Hospital Blue" on the wrapper. The color aggravates me because I know it has been chosen specifically to have "a calming effect" but it makes everything look cheap and hyper-artificial.

Down a fluorescently lit hallway are tiny bedrooms. Each girl has her own room except the four most recent newcomers. We occupy the "four-room", a room divided by waist-high sub-walls. Each space has a chair, desk and bed with a mattress no thicker than two inches sitting directly on a flimsy spring rack. There is only enough room to sit on the chair between the bed and desk.

No girl is allowed out of the four-room without standing at the door and asking "Permission to come out?" and then waiting for Staff in the office to yell back "Granted". If you forget to ask permission, you get a zero. Despite being 20 feet from the staff office, we often have to ask permission several times before Staff replies, probably to test our patience, or our subservience. Cottage is just as fucked as T.L.C, but we are more obedient. By sheer numbers, we could easily overpower them, but there is no fight left in us.

We are given a monthly credit to purchase shampoo, tampons, postage, yarn, snacks and cigarettes from the cottage office. If you don't write any letters, you can budget in an extra pack of cigarettes. Smoking, hygiene, art are all of equal value here. Spend wisely. Everything is tight.

Despite a limited budget, some girls discard their yarn if it gets unmanageably tangled. I keep it and find the task of untangling it therapeutic. Taking giant wads of mess and turning it into tidy balls of yarn is satisfying in its own way. The girls think I'm crazy, I think they're

167

lazy. The staff thinks I am manipulating the girls out of something of value and "working the system". I think I will make a blanket.

During socializing time we are allowed to play cards, read or crochet. Smoking is allowed if you are 15 years old and Phase 1; only girls on Phase 4 are allowed to carry lighters. In here, the power to light another girl's cigarette is like having the power to heal. Without a Phase 4, we have to ask the staff or take a bump off another girl's cigarette. A bump leaves you beholden to that girl, because it wastes one precious puff of her cigarette.

"You knocked my cherry off my cigarette! Don't you know how to take a bump?"

"I don't want to be partners with Heidi, I want to be partners with someone else!"

Rages and outbursts are daily occurrences, but no matter how I try to steel myself, prepare for the impending emotional explosion, I'm still taken off guard. Like an earthquake.

I don't know why these girls act so tough but then blow up about meaningless things. How can someone who is in here for stabbing her sister with a fucking knife cry to Staff because she didn't get her special seat on the couch during T.V. time?

The mood of Cottage changes in waves. I'm sensitive to the group mood and feel when there is harmony, or tension. I have been doing my best to accomplish detachment.

"No one ever lets me play Spades with them!" Heidi is yelling to no one in particular, loudly enough so no one can ignore her. She has red hair and her eyes look squinty and mean no matter what her mood, because she is so fat. She looks older than most because of her size, but, like me, she is one of the youngest girls here.

"We're in the middle of a game right now, we're not going to stop." Maxi, a tough Samoan girl from Hawaii tries to reason with her, which is always an impossibility.

"I want to play Spades too, but no one ever lets me be their partner," another girl, Linda, says.

"May I go down to my room and write?" I ask Staff. I want to avoid the explosion that is about to happen. *Can't anyone else feel it coming?* When Staff allows me to go to my room and write for the remaining thirty minutes of social time, I feel I've been granted shelter from a storm.

The tension and voices escalate up the hall.

Linda, whitewashed, chubby, and puffy, whose body looks like it's never left the couch, is sent to her room for a timeout. Hers is directly across from the four room, and we are not allowed to close our doors, leaving me as the only person she can seek attention from. She's making the sounds of someone who's lost control, but I see Linda looking up, stealing glimpses to see if I'm paying attention. I won't feel sorry for her; she's invading my moment of peace. I don't believe she is actually suffering, I think that her thick dark hair doesn't match her white skin. Her narrow, naïve eyes rub me the wrong way with their stupidity, now bloodshot and swollen from the trauma she is causing herself.

If I involve myself in her drama, I could get a zero for what Staff calls "feeding into her behavior". I do my best to ignore her, but I can't help looking over when she becomes quiet. Linda is sitting on the floor and has cut her wrist with some piece of something. Once she knows I've seen her, the screaming starts up again and her narrow, mousy eyes rest on me.

"Permission to come out?" I scream up the hall. Linda's hysterics drown out my mundane request. Our eyes locked in a dare.

"Permission to come out?" I yell with exaggerated indifference, looking into her sloppy wet eyes as they plead for attention.

"Permission granted." The words are tossed down the hall like a key, releasing me from my room.

I take the two steps and stand at Linda's door. She's bleeding, but I've seen worse.

"Knock it off," I tell her. "Go to the bathroom and wrap some paper towels around your wrist and stop howling. We both know you aren't gonna get to die from this." I'm not breaking a rule to drag her out of her room. Why get us both in trouble because she is barely bleeding. Let her bleed. She did this to herself because she couldn't play cards. I'm not getting a zero. I'm on the verge of being off Phase One and getting my own room. If Linda keeps this up I'll probably get hers.

I walk to the common room and Maxi asks if I want to play Spades. As she deals me in, I look over at another girl's notebook cover.

What you see here
What you hear here
When you leave here
Let it stay here.

She says it's a quote from her Ala-something meeting.

It will be my new mantra until the day I get out. I am no longer looking to escape these buildings, but I plan to escape their hurt. I will allow them to think they've filled my mind with whatever they want, as long as I can get out of here. I promise to believe it all, memorize all their dogma and regurgitate it like my very own. But when I leave here, let it stay here.

My parents brought me here to erase the things they don't understand; this institution is their magic wand to wave all of it away. I can become an entirely different person. What was so great about me anyway? You want to know what's worse than not going to gigs or getting to dye your hair? Being locked in a room alone for three days with nothing but your helpless thoughts. Want to know what is worse than the idiots at high school? The crazy people you come to know and love in a locked youth center.

I don't ever want anyone to have control over me again. I will be autonomous some day. I learned that word here, just like the poem.

Music Saves Lives

♫ ♪ ♫ ♪ ♫ ♪ ♫ ♪ ♫ ♪ ♫ ♪ ♫

Thank You

♫ ♪ ♫ ♪ ♫ ♪ ♪ ♫ ♪ ♫ ♪ ♫

SOUNDTRACK

Song	Artist	Album
Can't Put Your Arms Around a Memory	Johnny Thunders	So Alone
Clampdown	The Clash	London's calling
Never Going Back Again	Fleetwood Mac	Rumors
I Love Little Girls	Oingo Boingo	Only a Lad
Fuck Authority	Wasted Youth	Regan's in
Problem Child	Wasted Youth	Regan's in
Mesopotamia	B-52'S	Mesopotamia
No Values	Black Flag	Jealous Again
We Destroy the Family	Fear	The Record
I Am Right	Saccharine Trust	Paganicons
Living in Darkness	Agent Orange	Living in Darkness
Train in Vain	The Clash	London's Calling
Holiday in Cambodia	Dead Kennedy's	Fresh Fruit for Rotting Vegetables
Too Young to Die	Agent Orange	Living in Darkness
I Need Somebody	Iggy Pop	Raw Power
Wild in the Streets	Circle Jerks	Rodney on the Roq
Lude Boy	Social Distortion	Hell Comes to your House
Telling Them	Social Distortion	Hell Comes to your House
Reject Yourself	100 flowers	Hell Comes to your House
We're Only Gonna Die	Bad Religion	How Could Hell Be Any Worse?
Platinum Blonde	Blondie	
Citadel	Redd Kross	Teen Babes from Monsanto
Some Girls	Rolling Stones	Some Girls
I Don't Wanna Be Like That	Joe Jackson	Look Sharp
Gotta Getaway	Stiff Little Fingers	Nobody's Heroes

Because this story wouldn't have happened without the music, and because the music set the stage for everything we did, I wanted to list the "Soundtrack to the Book." There are references to lyrics and songs throughout the book that I hope I don't have to remove for any reason. This is not an attempt to plagiarize, but a nod to artists that changed my life. I hope some people get turned on to these old albums and BUY each one because (to quote Mike Watt) "Punk Rock Changed Our Lives".

ACKNOWLEDGMENTS

This is where I get to say thank you to all the people who helped me. There are a lot.

Thanks to Mom and Dad, I was a tough kid to have and you did the best you could. I wish I could take away all the hurt, I know that you do too.

Thanks to Serena Dank for trying to teach me how to communicate with my parents. Thanks for trying to help so many people, despite all the shit you got from everyone.

As for Jack, I suppose I should find something clever to say here about all the things, good and bad, that we went through. But now, all I can say is—"We will remember the laughter."

Deborah, if this book makes it to you somehow, please know that you were instrumental to my survival. Thank you.

Thanks to Debbie R. for saying "You should write a book" on the day when I was truly ready to hear it. Thank you Evil Bob for driving me to Beyond Baroque writers group and sitting with me week after week until I was comfortable enough to go on my own. Thank you to everyone at the B.B. writers group, especially Tom Frolic, Karen, and Ida. Thank you to Angie for talking me down when I wanted to cover this with gas and set it on fire. Thank you to Kim B. and Charlotte B. Stanley for the editing.

Thank you Carol, for straightening me out and setting me back on track.

To the people of the Texture Villa who graciously adopted me, Thank you, especially their youngest angel; D-Nice.

Thank you Barrett for being my best friend forever and for doing your best to keep me sane.

Thank you Duke. Your unbridled and often unwarranted faith in me is the glue that keeps me together.

Thank you Jessica, Dustin and Chris, if you read this book, I am sorry. At least now you understand me when I tell you that our family is my happy ending. It has all been worth it.

Cover photo: the very first time I ran away, as documented by RJP.

ABOUT THE AUTHOR

When this happened years ago, I thought my story unique.

Now I'm old and I know how common it is.

Summon your courage friends. Speak your truth.

K.P. - age 52 ½

Made in the USA
Monee, IL
21 August 2020

39132371R00111